Ask And You Shall
Receive

Dearest Kayla,

may God continue to fill
your life with blessings and
abundance!

With Love and Gratitude,

Receive Joy

Receive Joy

Rediscover Truth

Though the information within the pages is researched and documented, it is a reference book for educational purpose only. The information is *not* intended to prescribe treatment or *cure* conditions. The reader shall be made aware that this information is *not* intended as medical advice and *not* intended to be used in place of medical treatment. It is merely the sharing of knowledge and information from the research and experience of the author. The reader is strongly encouraged to do further research. If medical *problems* are prevalent and persist, please consult your doctor. You are highly encouraged to make your own health care decisions, based upon your own research, along with your health care professional. You are totally responsible for your own self if you choose to do anything based on what you have learned within these pages.

Ask And You Shall Receive
Receive Joy

Receive Joy Publishing
Naples, Florida, U.S.A.

ISBN: 978-0-9988484-8-8
Library of Congress Control Number: 2017905351

Receive Joy, Naples, FL
www.receivejoy.com
ask@receivejoy.com

DEDICATION

This book is dedicated to the Trinity:
God, Jesus, and The Holy Spirit.

CONTENTS

Part One—Ask!

Part Two—Seek!

Contents

A NOTE FROM THE EDITOR

A book editor's work is akin to that of the lighting and sound tech in the theatre—when we do our work correctly, we quietly exist.

So it is a sincere pleasure to be asked by Receive Joy to step out from the shadows and say a few words about this book. First and foremost, it is clear that it is written from a place of Passion, Knowledge, and Experience. The excellent writing and the obvious time that went into editing by Receive Joy's circle of previous readers let me concentrate on a deep edit. My job was to make excellent even better.

The numerous real-life examples you will read (many times, if you are like me) balance well with the How-To sections and the positivity that courses throughout the pages infuses the book with an energy of purposeful pace that also gives abundant time to absorb and apply the ideas and exercises.

From a personal point of view, the contents of this book have already begun working in my life. I am practicing what is prescribed and seeing results.

Having been the first male to read the book, I found it to speak clearly to me. The male penchant for practical solutions and clear instructions is certainly met.

The precepts and ideas in the book are familiar from the works of teachers like Wayne Dyer, Caroline Myss, and Ram Dass, yet they are presented in such a way as to be brand new. No one, in my extensive study of both spiritual practices and storytelling, has focused so clearly on the Word, the all-important Logos.

Receive Joy set the intention to write a book that is "light and easy." When asked if they had succeeded, I replied: "Tremendously so! It has Air, Space, Peace, and Love infused in it."

This book was a great gift that came at the perfect time in my life. I know it will be the same for you.

—Joey Madia
    Editor, screenwriter, playwright, novelist,
       and teacher.
    Beaufort, NC April 2017

A NOTE FROM THE TEXTUAL EDITOR

To edit someone's book is to be invited into their lives in depth—always a rewarding experience, because you learn about yourself as well as the writer.

"Ask and You Shall Receive" offered a singular opportunity to see the empowering and uplifting spirit that both Carisa and Sylvia embody, and to come away with some of their practices, as I know I shall.

One of the things I appreciated most in working with Receive Joy was their appreciation for the power of words, and their attention to that power being used in a positive way. We can all learn so much from that single example.

If some of its concepts of positive statements and the reinforcement of intentions verbally and in writing sound familiar, the authors' experience with those precepts bring them up to date with very personal stories that can translate to others' experience in 21st century spirituality. Their use of meditation to reset the mind, and their helpful concepts such as Five Minute Couch Time, are balm for the busy lives we lead in these times.

My hope as a text editor is that the readers benefit fully from the abundance of inspiration and practical, positive ideas these two authors offer.

—Harriet Howard Heithaus
Textual editor, journalist, copy editor
Naples, FL April 2017

A NOTE FROM THE AUTHOR

This book will help encourage you to create and define a direction and plan for your life. My heartfelt intention is for readers to feel abundantly encouraged with the desire to:

- ♥ Receive joy, be happy, have fun, and celebrate
- ♥ Be connected to God
- ♥ Declare with faith
- ♥ Dominate your life
- ♥ Have an aligned heart and mind
- ♥ Focus and ask
- ♥ Love yourself
- ♥ Be fulfilled with love and gratitude
- ♥ Exercise a conscious mind through the use of clear thoughts and positive words
- ♥ Pray and meditate often
- ♥ Rediscover the truth

Ask And You Shall Receive

All of the stories in this book are true. They are the real life happenings of family and friends. I chose to base this book only on genuine accounts to share the awareness that our entire lives are made up of many continuous conscious, miraculous creations.

Every word in this book is positive and will bless you. Repeated word phrases such as "let us" have been used on purpose as a reassuring incantation to build welcoming encouragement and adventure on a new path in your life. Through the intentional use of positive words, I desire to create a hypnotic rhythm forming a harmonious imprint on our subconscious. Simply reading this book will lift you to a stronger frequency that shall open your awareness. Please allow yourself to joyfully receive some unique word choices. However, to give examples of old patterns, there are words I prefer to mute, so they will be in a smaller size and italic.

I write with the divine purpose to be God's continual stream of love and glory, sharing joy with myself and all the world. I desire for humanity to be reset to the divine love and perfection that we already are while experiencing true happiness and health through love and gratitude. Let us Rediscover the Truth.

Rejoice and enjoy!
With Love and Gratitude,
Receive Joy

"**Ask**, and it will be given to you; **seek** and you will find; **knock** and the door will be opened to you. For everyone who asks receives; the one who seeks finds; and to the one who knocks, the door will be opened."

—Matthew 7:7-8 (NIV)

INTRODUCTION

I grew up a happy kid from the Midwest. I did well in school, loved to participate in sports, and played an instrument. I sang in choir, went to church on Sundays, read the Bible and loved the Lord with all my heart, mind, and soul for as long as I can remember. My greatest joy was to share what I had with others, find the good in people, and have fun.

Life has always been **light and easy** for me, as the verse from the Holy Bible offers.

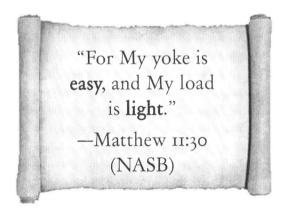

"For My yoke is **easy,** and My load is **light.**"
—Matthew 11:30 (NASB)

Ask And You Shall Receive

As my life progressed, I began to notice that **light and easy** was far from the norm for the majority of the population. This greatly perplexed me.

Why is life a true blessing for me and yet for many others it appears to be a series of challenging events? It seems as if I am speaking directly to and communicating with God and His Universe in real time while others require a translator. I often wonder, why do so few people use the Power of the Universe daily?

Please ask yourself:

Do you perceive your life as light and easy?

Do you have resources available to plug into that empower you in every moment?

Do you receive what you desire?

Do you ask constantly for what you wish?

What if I were to tell you that the Universe we live in already has powerful resources set up for you to use continually for free?

Introduction

When I was 17 years old, a miraculous experience left me with an understanding of God's Almighty Power and how to use it to guide my life.

It was around 10 p.m. and I was sitting comfortably on the couch watching TV when I felt the heat of an intense light on my face. A blinding light illuminated the whole room; a light so bright I thought a Hollywood spotlight must have been shining in on me from outside the window.

Out of curiosity, I was drawn toward the window. When I moved the thick, heavy drape, only darkness lay outside. Questions raced through my mind. How was the room glowing with the intense brightness of the sun? What was the source and the meaning of this great light that overtook me and the room? Was there a message in this light?

Looking back, it proved to me that we are connected with a great Light Source. This is the wisdom that I desire to share with the world.

On my 50th birthday, I decided to give a loving gift to the world. I wish to empower humankind by showing everyone how easy it is to communicate with the Ether when we speak its language. The Ether is the vast continual power all around us. All is possible all the time, just as Jesus himself promised us in the Holy Bible:

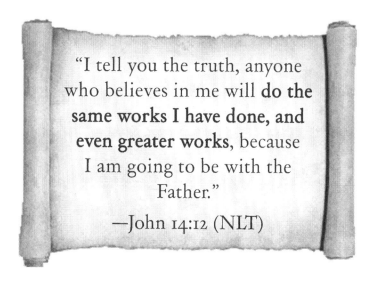

"I tell you the truth, anyone who believes in me will **do the same works I have done, and even greater works**, because I am going to be with the Father."

—John 14:12 (NLT)

". . . **with God all things are possible.**"
—Matthew 19:26 (KJV)

I have used these Power Sources of the Universe all my life and I write this book now to share with you the **Nine Step Method** that makes my life **light and easy**. I developed the Method for my family and friends so that we may all tap into the magnificent Power of the Universe. Now that we all use the Method and obtain the same results, I wish to share the Nine Steps to empower everyone to feel the freedom of a **light and easy** life.

To communicate with the Ether, we simply require the recipe to call upon and tap into this vast resource. Every recipe presented in a cookbook lists the ingredients with the exact amounts and easy-to-follow steps. Because the recipe has been perfected, the only requirement is to follow these proven steps and the end result turns out wonderful every time. May this book be your inspiration to enjoy and perfect your co-creation power.

Part One of the book will explain the setup of the Universe and give everyone an understanding of how our physical bodies communicate with the Divine Power. This Power is constantly present and available to everyone in any and every situation. This foundation enables us to easily use nine empowering steps.

In Part Two, I will present the Nine Step Method, which is the recipe to harness and make wonderful use of the Power of the Universe. These Nine Steps are the inspired pattern I developed to create my life exactly as I desire it to be.

Finally, in Part Three, I reveal powerful ways that enable us to go deeper into this practice and enhance the use of these Nine Steps and the Power explained in Part One.

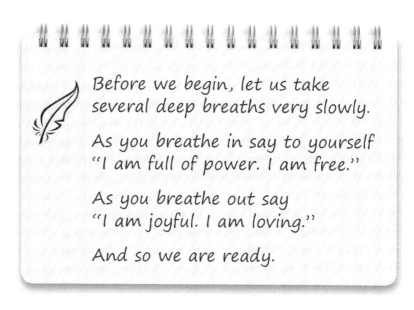

Before we begin, let us take several deep breaths very slowly.

As you breathe in say to yourself "I am full of power. I am free."

As you breathe out say "I am joyful. I am loving."

And so we are ready.

Open your heart and your mind now and journey with me to a new and more powerful, focused and loved, aware and connected, **light and easy** YOU!

Part One

Ask!

Chapter 1

THE POWER OF THE UNIVERSE

Look up. Look up at the sky. We see the blue. It is vast. There is so much more out there than what is underneath our feet and immediately around us. There is more than the air we breathe. There is an in-visible force that surrounds all. There is a Power. The Universe is full of Power.

We all come from this Power. It is greater than our individual self. It has continual abundance. It is **formulated from love**. It contains all light and life. It is magnificent; it is free; and it is equally available to all of us. It supports and embraces all life. Somehow, we have an inner knowledge that we are from this vast Heavenly Power containing continual awesome perfection.

It is a beautiful energy that exists and is full of absolute intelligence. It is consistent and flows progressively.

This Power is called many names: God, Holy Spirit, Holy Ghost, Spirit of God, Almighty Power, God Source, Source Light Energy, The Kingdom of Heaven, The Universe, The Quantum Field, The Morphic Field, Firmament, The Universal Energy, The Universal Force, Ether, The Heavenly Dimensions, The Divine, Outer Space, Worlds Beyond, and so on.

There are many words we use to describe this Power. How can we become more consciously aware of the Power? Let us be more mindful of the Divine Power so that we can access and call on it. We all agree that there is something powerful, tremendous, awesome, and mysterious out there which is greater than ourselves and part of ourselves. It is outside of us and it is inside of us. Although we sometimes feel we are separate from it, **we are indeed connected** to it. As it surrounds us, it literally fills the space between every cell of our body and it fills all matter.

When God flung the stars into existence, He set up a **divine delivery system**. Since we are His most valued creation, He wishes for us to be aware of it, understand it, access it, communicate with it, and use it in our daily lives for our greatest good. It is always fully available to us.

> "'Bring the whole tithe into the storehouse, that there may be food in my house. Test me in this,' says the Lord Almighty, 'and see if I will not throw **open the floodgates of heaven** and **pour out so much blessing** that there will not be room enough to store it.'"
>
> —Malachi 3:10 (NIV)

There is more than enough of everything for everyone. There is **absolute abundance**.

It is time to decide to open ourselves and our lives to **receive**. We have the choice to allow ourselves to **flow with this awesome force**. When God breathed into us His gift of life, we received connection to His Almighty Power. Let us embrace this Power. God gave us His Kingdom, which includes this Universe and all its Power, as our inheritance.

"Then the King will say to those on His right, 'Come, you who are blessed by my Father, **inherit the kingdom prepared for you** from the foundation of the world.'"

—Matthew 25:34 (NIV)

Let us decide to cash the check and use the wealth. Let us understand that the Heavenly Dimensions are here for us and that they support us. This Universal Energy is our divine gift, our birthright, given to us by God and our inheritance. The cosmos is carefully designed to please us, to help us, to make us happy, to give us everything we wish for and everything our heart desires.

It has been said many times in many ways: What we can conceive and believe, the Universe will help us to achieve. This Almighty Power was set up for our use: now it is time to learn its language and allow ourselves to use it.

The Power Of The Universe

One of my clients shared a story of swimming in the ocean. He was about a mile offshore, when all of a sudden a strong storm blew in. Although he was a triathlete, the waves were so forceful that he became too tired to make it back to shore. He began to feel greatly fatigued.

He told God that it was all right if this was his time to go. He started sinking. Instantly, he felt a big rock under his feet. He was able to stand on the rock as he saw his friends rowing a boat from shore. They had to pull him into the boat.

From that moment he knew there was a Power watching over him.

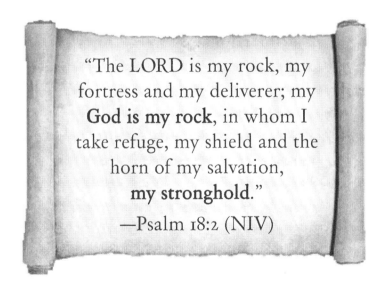

"The LORD is my rock, my fortress and my deliverer; my **God is my rock**, in whom I take refuge, my shield and the horn of my salvation, **my stronghold.**"
—Psalm 18:2 (NIV)

God, the Almighty Power of the Universe, **is always with us**. His Power is right here to call upon especially when we seek him most.

Fourteen years ago, I was sitting at my desk at work and I realized I desired new Rolodex cards. I had gone to the office supply store four times, and every time I had forgotten to buy Rolodex cards. At that moment, I looked up to God and said, "Your memory is superior to mine. Please remind me about the Rolodex cards tomorrow."

When I came to work the next morning at 7 a.m., there were two large metal boxes leaning against the door blocking my entry. Surprised, I picked up the two tin boxes, took them inside and set them on my desk. When I opened them up, they were large cases full of Rolodex cards the size of automobile license plates. This was the first time I had seen such a thing. I laughed and thanked God. God has such a **sense of humor**! I will remember Rolodex cards for the rest of my life.

God created us in His image. He also laughs and smiles as humans do and creates grand things with His sense of humor. He often uses humor when giving us what we **ask** for. Let us create more with joyous **laughter, smiles, and humor**.

He continues to surprise me with His wit on many occasions. I came out of work one day to find a brand new dumpster gently resting against the back bumper of my car. I wondered where the dumpster came from and why it was resting against my car. As always, I asked myself, "What did I ask for in my last prayer?"

I immediately remembered that I had blocked the trash bin at my apartment building so that the cans had remained full all week. I asked the Universe to find a solution as to where to put my trash. God gave me an enormous answer—and a reminder to **use this free, abundant, perfect Power of the Universe**.

Chapter 2

THE POWER OF
THE QUANTUM WORLD

The Quantum World consists of what lies beyond our physical perception and conception. It is the in-visible.

To make it easy to envision, compare it with the Internet. In order to transmit and receive anything on our computers and cell phones (free of wires), waves travel to and from our devices via cell towers. Our bodies are like cell towers, emitting and receiving waves that travel through the air. Similar to the waves emitted from a cell phone or X-ray machine, they all are in-visible.

Our minds and our hearts receive and transmit. The waves they send out can penetrate all physical matter. These waves hold a consistent strength and amount of energy over any distance and can be received instantly anywhere in the world. They are more powerful and more accurate than the waves radiating from any manufactured objects such as radio beams or satellite transmissions.

The mind can transmit, receive, and change any frequency that exists. The exact frequency we send out, or transmit, attracts back a matching energy. These waves connect us with the universal divine delivery system.

We function like magnetic frequency generators. We come equipped with two major energy generators to connect to the Power Source: our mind and our heart—our heart being the more powerful. Interestingly, research at the HeartMath Institute in Boulder Creek, California, revealed that the heart has an electric force 100 times stronger and a magnetic force 5,000 times stronger than the brain.

Our hearts create frequency vibrations through our feelings just as our minds create frequency vibrations through our thoughts. The heart is first to develop during gestation in the womb, and when fully grown contains about 40,000 neurons.

Ask And You Shall Receive

Once I was sitting in the Jacuzzi of a wonderful hotel where I was staying with friends to celebrate my birthday, I was thinking a pleasant thought of having a drink in my hand. I usually pass on alcoholic beverages; still, in this very instant I had the opportunity to look like a movie star or model in a fancy hotel advertisement.

Just a few minutes later, one of my friends came to the Jacuzzi carrying two margaritas. **A thought generated a vibration which instantly materialized.**

Years later when I asked her how she knew what I was requesting, she told me that we had received two free margarita coupons from the hotel. I thought, she chose margaritas because we had vacationed together years ago in the Florida Keys and had enjoyed margaritas at Jimmy Buffett's Margaritaville.

The Universe "hears" our requests and acts on them.

Our mind and thought processes are independent of our physical brain. The flesh of our brain is part of our physical body. It registers all sensations. For example, it is attached to the nervous system, which makes the heart beat. The vessel itself lacks thought process. Our whole body, including the physical brain, is entirely controlled by our mind. The mind is so powerful that it can override all systems in the body. We may think, "Why is my body reacting this way?" when actually the body does what the mind tells it to do and our body feels what the mind focuses on. Emotion is absent from the physical body. It is the mind that is in charge of all feelings and the processing of sensations.

We are eternal beings with physical bodies, living within a Quantum World. As we are vibrational beings, we oscillate at the same vibration with God. We all live vibrationally connected by our matching frequencies to His abundant Source of Energy. Filled with this Source Energy, we are always vibrating with it.

This abundant Source Energy contains a constant understanding and honoring of all life forms. It is reactive to us. Our **thoughts, focus, feelings, and words continually summon this energy**. It is all-providing and all-loving, full of continual possibilities.

When we are aligned with the perfect vibration of love and joy, we are connected with God's Universal Energy. In this Light, all is well. When we choose to match our vibrational power to the Almighty Power, we regain our birthright. Our birthright is to be consciously connected with God's Power Source, allowing us throughout our lives to flow **light and easy**.

Is Life Force consciously connected? Are we one big entity with separate outlets? **Humanity is a Collective Consciousness.** In his books, Napoleon Hill refers to it as "The Master Mind." Roger D. Nelson and his colleagues from the Princeton Engineering Anomalies Research (PEAR) Institute, associated with Princeton University, refer to it as "Coherent Consciousness."

The institute conducted a continual nine-year study called "The Global Consciousness Project." The study included people from 37 different countries worldwide. Electrodes were used to measure and track brain wave frequencies. When I met Roger D. Nelson, he explained to me that prior to a major incident—a tsunami or "9/11"—the brain wave patterns of everyone tested in every country rose off the charts simultaneously.

I bought a computer from an acquaintance of mine in Germany to run a special software program. It sat dormant for a while. When my friend visited, she asked to use the computer. We both were trying to remember the password. She sent an email to the former owner in Germany, hoping he remembered the password.

The next morning our German friend from whom I bought the computer called. I said, "Thank you for calling, did you receive our email?" He replied, "What email?" Usually, we only talk twice a year. He was calling me about a completely different matter. Our intention of talking to him was so strong that the Universe compelled him to instantly connect.

How often do we think about a person and they call a moment later and likewise, how many times do we call someone and the first thing they say to us is, "I was just thinking about you"?

Once a mind conceptualizes or experiences something, all minds can conceive the same thing in the same moment. This is why numerous inventions are made at the same time. Here are a few examples:

Thomas Edison (1847–1931) and Joseph Swan (1828–1914) simultaneously developed the light bulb based on carbon fiber. Carl Benz (1844–1929) and Gottlieb Daimler (1834–1900) developed the automobile at the same time in 1885, both in Germany, one in Mannheim, the other in Stuttgart. Elisha Grey (1835–1901) and Alexander Graham Bell (1847–1922) both developed the telephone at the same time. Bell is credited today as the developer of the telephone because he announced the patent two hours earlier than Grey on February 14, 1878.

The same phenomenon is shown when an athlete achieves a record time and it becomes the new standard for all humans in that field. The new record time will then quickly be achieved by many athletes and often surpassed.

If one rat completes a maze in a certain time, later other rats can reach the end of the maze more quickly. Once a new neural pathway is created, all life forms can instantly tap into it and follow it.

After 30 years of studying and working with Quantum Physics and the laws of nature, I have observed and now understand how all humanity is connected. Quantum Physics includes the study of subatomic particles and electromagnetic waves.

We are most powerful when our brain waves are in balance. Our whole body is a finely tuned instrument, functioning optimally when in balance. There are many techniques to harmonize brain waves through conditioning and to balance them to their intrinsic, optimal patterns such as meditation, yoga, biofeedback, light therapy, and music therapy.

Every cell has a unique frequency. We can recharge and encourage every cell to resonate at its perfect energy state. Humans have the ability to affect the intelligence of every individual cell. When we keep the vibrational balance in all parts of our body, everything is possible.

We vibrate with God's divine Source Light Energy. Every cell in our body is bursting with photon light energy. We are light beings with magnificent intelligence vibrating in every cell. This is God's Power within us.

Chapter 3

THE POWER OF THE MIND

The Universe acts as our divine delivery system. As with gravity, whether we believe it exists or we lack the belief in this universal principle, it just is and it constantly works. With every thought we think, and even more with every word we speak, we create by using this delivery system.

This delivering force is absolute and eternal. It prevails. All we have to do is to make "the choice to decide" to utilize this Power to our advantage. We were given this life and this Power to create. Like our Heavenly Father, **we are creators, inviters, and attractors of all things in our lives**.

"Be careful how
you think; your life
is shaped by your
thoughts."
—Proverbs 4:23 (GNT)

Can one human being influence and change many things? The answer is a definite yes. Throughout history, we have numerous examples of one human being having a vision and focusing on it. When they completely surrendered to their desired outcome in a peaceful and positive way, all change began. Positive examples are: Mahatma Gandhi, Nelson Mandela, Mother Teresa, Nicola Tesla, Thomas Edison, Henry Ford, Bill Gates, and Steve Jobs.

Now take a look into your mirror. What do you notice? Is there anything you desire to change? What is the first step necessary to change anything?

Ask And You Shall Receive

To change anything, let us first change our minds. The mind is a powerful creator; so powerful that it is the source that convinces us to do everything.

Before any change is possible, we shall consciously welcome in the opportunity to improve our thought processes. Change starts with our mind. Change happens when we focus our awareness on what we truly desire and start to target what brings us the most joy.

Let us decide to focus on receiving happiness and what makes our heart sing. It is self-caring and self-nurturing to keep our focus there. Let us **always focus on the solution**. Especially when we pray, let us pray into the positive desired outcome. Let us **ask** for our desires and act as if they are already here.

Ask, Ask, Ask!

The four **components of focusing our thoughts** are:

1. **Think** it, **speak** it, and **write** it as if we have it already.

2. **Visualize** ourselves with our goal in every detail.

3. **Affirm** and **anchor** the desired achievement in our mind and heart.

4. Adopt a **positive attitude** and **celebrate** the desired achievement.

What we focus on and constantly think about, we attract. To use this powerful resource, we shall hold our attention on what we prefer. **Focus only on the good**. Let us feel great as we attract our creations.

When we have tapped into God's Power and have increased our focused consciousness, only then can we create more in a year than we can accomplish by drifting through our entire life with lack of purpose. The method to accomplish this greatness is as follows:

1. **Think** many identical thoughts of our desires.

2. **Stay** with these thoughts; hold them and ponder them for more than a minute at a time.

3. **Revisit** these empowering thoughts as often as you wish.

Let us give the thought a chance to anchor deeply in our mind and create new neural pathways. A **neural pathway** is a series of neurons connected together forming a path that enables a signal to be sent from one region of the brain to another.

Two years after my father passed away, my mother came to our house and **asked** my husband if he knew a suitable man for her to date. After 45 years of marriage, she wished for company. My husband replied, "There is only one guy I know your age who is single. He is over there sitting on the couch." This gentleman had been a friend of the family for many years, and my mother already knew him well. He had been single his whole life and had come to a number of our family gatherings.

"Really? That is John!" she answered. My husband replied, "Yes, you **asked** for a single man and he is the only one I know." They have now been happily married for 10 years. My mother opened her heart and changed her mind toward him.

When we **ask**, the Universe answers. It answers in many ways and some of them are surprising. Let us open our minds and hearts to receive what we **ask** for.

After our dog collar had gone missing multiple times, I often **asked** my youngest daughter to help me find it and she always did. Before she went to bed, she **focused** on it being found.

In the mornings she knew where it was. On one

occasion, it was lying under her bed; another time she knew exactly where to look in the lake—there it was, lying in the shallow water.

Asking with a determined focus on the preferred result, and with a clear **intention** to receive what the Universe answers, creates amazing results. Have faith in the power of intention.

My younger sister **asked** for a rain jacket for Christmas. I called her and **asked** her to describe her perfect jacket to me. This built our excitement and desire to have it. I **asked** God to honor her Christmas request for my sake of having the perfect gift for her to make her happy. She desired it to be purple, have a hood, hang below the waist, and be waterproof. I added as a parameter for it to be on sale.

When my older sister and my mother went Christmas shopping, they looked in many stores before they made their last stop at Columbia Outfitters to buy this perfect jacket. My mother was ready to go home and they almost passed the store, when my sister insisted they go inside, because she knew it was there.

They decided to stop in with the clear **asking and receiving intention** of having the right jacket, and found it on sale. It was hip-length, waterproof, with a hood, and purple. The Universe always answers.

Ask And You Shall Receive

Let us organize our thoughts, set clear intentions, focus on our intention, **ask**, and be open to **receive** the delivery from the Universe.

Chapter 4

THE POWER OF ATTRACTING

Every vibration that radiates out of us in the form of thought, word, and deed is a form of asking and **by the Law of the Universe comes back**. This is the only possibility. We often refer to this drawing effect as the Law of Attraction, the Golden Rule, Karma, the Boomerang Effect, Like Attracts Like, and so on. The basic principle behind all of them is similar: our thoughts, words, and deeds cause matching reactions.

The human mind is a magnetic force, drawing toward it everything we focus on: consciously or subconsciously, positive or negative, of good intention or the lack thereof. Every thought that goes out receives a matching returned vibrational answer. The answer is automatically summoned to us.

This magnetic attraction is our creation power. I imagine my life as living in a hall of mirrors; inside are only me and our creator—and He only creates good.

Everything in our lives reflects right back at us. Every good that goes out of us comes right back, as does everything else. Let us choose to radiate what is good, kind, blessed, loving, encouraging, and uplifting.

God gave us creation power. He created us; and everything around us.

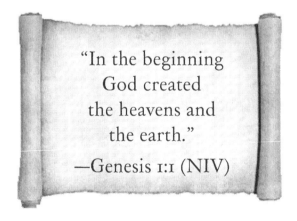

"In the beginning
God created
the heavens and
the earth."
—Genesis 1:1 (NIV)

"So **God created mankind
in His own image,** in the
image of God He created
them; male and female
He created them."
—Genesis 1:26 (NIV)

God loves us so much that He desired us to be
co-creators with the great I AM. To do this, He
created a Universal Power and designed us to be able
to tap into and harness that power. It is here for the
asking. And so we shall **ask.**

Let us decide now to consciously create good
and glorify God with His eternal absolute Law of
Attraction. Let us give full praise to God for setting
up His powerful divine delivery system. Human
prosperity is based on this absolute law.

> "But whose delight is in the **law of the LORD**, and who meditates on his law day and night. That person is like a tree planted by streams of water, which yields its fruit in season and whose leaf does not wither—**whatever they do prospers.**"
>
> —Psalm 1:2-3 (NIV)

Does this mean we co-create everything? Yes, we do create everything in our reality. We create with our thoughts and words and then our actions follow.

A woman in her forties was having financial challenges and recently found herself single again. Since she desired to make positive changes in her life, she decided that attracting wealth to her was to be her first step.

She visualized herself as a rich woman and posted sticky notes all around her house saying: I am rich. Money flows easily. I am a millionaire. A few months later she married again. This time, she married one of the wealthiest men in town. Applying her **conscious creation power**, she currently lives the happy, wealthy life of her dreams.

A friend of mine once gave her mother's diamond ring to her future son-in-law to be redesigned into a ring for her daughter. At their engagement party, the couple was playing volleyball and the stone fell out of the setting into the grass. A few hours later, her daughter noticed it missing.

It was dark when the party ended and her Mom said, "Let's go home and we will come back in the morning and find the diamond." The next day, the mother and the couple went out to look for the stone in the big yard. The mother told the groom, "Walk to the tree and you will find the diamond in the grass under the tree."

As he came back, he told her, "You were right. It was sitting in the grass under the tree." My friend decided that the diamond was to be found wherever she desired to **consciously create** it.

Prior to her surgery, a friend wished for a particular doctor who was the best in his field for this type of procedure. The doctor was over 80 years old and ready to retire. Miraculously, she was his last patient.

She decided to reward herself, for her successful surgery, with a leather jacket. On the way home, she stopped by her neighborhood leather store. Out front was a sale rack with one leather jacket on it. She put on the jacket, it fit perfectly and she had the exact amount of money in her pocket to buy it.

Let us use focused intention for creating things in all areas of our life. Remember, **the Universe pulls from all abundance**. It is already set up to deliver.

Imagine the Universe continuously coming to us with truckloads full of resources and yearning to deliver it. In order to find room to restock, the Universe eagerly off-loads everything day and night. Let us call in our orders so that the trucks can drop off whatever we wish at our door on an ongoing basis.

In one of our Miracle Group meetings (discussed in detail in Part Three), we talked about what we attracted during the previous week. A relatively new member of our group shared with us that, since she is now more aware of her creations, they are appearing in absolute abundance. She started to notice it when a co-worker of hers **asked** for a pen. Later that day, a bag of 150 donated pens came in to the charity for which she works.

She put the pens on her co-worker's desk. When he saw them, he was surprised and asked her what this bag of pens was doing on his table. She calmly said, "These are the pens you **asked** the Universe for." He had already forgotten about his order and was very surprised. **See your win and take it in.**

The next day, the same co-worker was seeking a Tide laundry pen to clean spots from clothes that were donated. He then jokingly said, "Now I ask the Universe to also deliver a Tide pen." When they came to the bottom of the bag full of donated clothes, there actually was a pack of laundry pens. The co-workers both had a thankful laugh about it.

Later in the week, she **asked** the Universe for one travel coffee mug, since now it was her turn to receive. Soon thereafter, a bag of 50 travel coffee cups was donated. Although she had just asked for one, she realized that **we can ask for more as well** and pass the rest on.

The universe is full of abundance. Why ask for a cup of water when we can have the whole river?

At the next meeting, the same member shared with us the following story: "I woke up one morning and my toilet was leaking. As I was laughing about this, with confident creation power, I **asked** God and His Universe for help."

"The next day, a brand new toilet showed up

donated at my job. My boss smiled and said we only sell clothing and home goods here. I told him that I can use this toilet! He was happy to pass on the donation to me."

Becoming more aware and confident, now owning her conscious creation power, she was able to take her win home.

We all can recall situations when we used attraction power with purpose. One common use is to attract a parking spot. We may start talking to ourselves saying, "There is an open spot for me." Soon enough we attract a spot.

Everyone creates consciously and *un*consciously at times. Let us lean on the House of the Great "I AM" more often and use His spiritual delivery system consciously for everything that we request and call into our lives.

Even if God's mighty Law of Attracting is new to us, we seem to have a built-in knowledge and awareness of it at times when something becomes very important to us. For example, after we buy a new car, the next few weeks we notice the same model and color car everywhere, because we have a fresh awareness.

Our focus directs our energy.

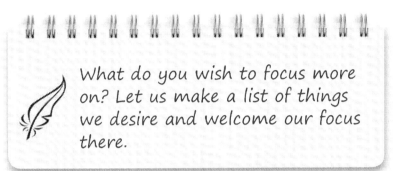

What do you wish to focus more on? Let us make a list of things we desire and welcome our focus there.

We all may wish for more joy in our lives. To attract and receive joy, simply choose to align with God's original blessed declaration that **all is good**. Let us choose to focus on our birthright of seeing the goodness in all creation. All is well all the time.

On the first page of the Bible, when God created everything, He saw that all was good all the time.

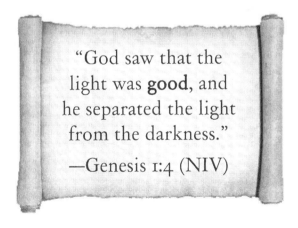

"God saw that the light was **good**, and he separated the light from the darkness."

—Genesis 1:4 (NIV)

"God called the dry ground 'land,' and the gathered waters he called 'seas.' And God saw that it was **good**."

—Genesis 1:10 (NIV)

"The land produced vegetation: plants bearing seed according to their kinds and trees bearing fruit with seed in it according to their kinds. And God saw that it was **good**."

—Genesis 1:12 (NIV)

"to govern the day
and the night, and to
separate light from
darkness. And God saw
that it was **good**."

—Genesis 1:18 (NIV)

"So God created the great
creatures of the sea and every
living thing with which the water
teems and that moves about in it,
according to their kinds, and every
winged bird according to its kind.
And God saw that it was **good**."

—Genesis 1:21 (NIV)

"God made the wild animals according to their kinds, the livestock according to their kinds, and all the creatures that move along the ground according to their kinds. And God saw that it was **good**."

—Genesis 1:25 (NIV)

". . . God saw all that he had made, and it was **very good**."

—Genesis 1:31 (NIV)

Because God focuses on the good, let us choose to direct our focus there as well. If **focusing on the good** is good enough for Him, then focusing on the good is good enough for me.

"This is the message we have heard from him and declare to you: **God is light**; in him there is no darkness at all."

—I John 1:5 (NIV)

During a visit with my extended family, I was listening to an elderly gentleman fill me in on what he was up to since I last saw him. He went on and on with his sad stories. As for me, life is good all the time.

I interrupted him and asked him straight on, "What is good in your life?" His eyes opened wide as he looked at me. It took him a moment to gather his thoughts before he answered, "You are right. There are good things. My grandchildren are a pure joy."

I encouraged him to tell me about the joy in his life and asked him to share only his good stories when we next meet.

First, **God declared that all is good seven times and then he blessed us**.

"God **blessed** them . . ."
—Genesis 1:28 (NIV)

He blessed us again when Jesus died. He left us **His** Holy Spirit.

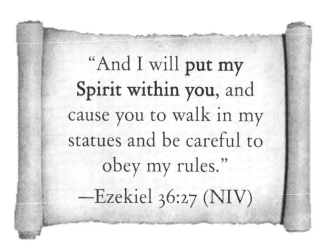

"And I will **put my Spirit within you**, and cause you to walk in my statues and be careful to obey my rules."
—Ezekiel 36:27 (NIV)

Because now His powerful Spirit is in us, we are the magnetic force operating within the vibrational field of attraction.

"... I am **filled
with power**, with
the Spirit of the
LORD ..."
—Micah 3:8 (NIV)

Imagine if we consciously **ask** all the time. Let us choose to use our focus intentionally and purify our thoughts and our words. Seek to find the **good** in everyone and everything, allowing our actions to create happiness and all the positive outcomes we desire.

Chapter 5

THE POWER OF RECEIVING AND GIVING

In accordance with the strongest law in the Universe, the Law of Attraction, the more one gives in joy, the more one receives. Giving and receiving share the same vibrational field as does flow and allow. Human nature is made to receive and give.

To begin to receive, the suggestion has been made to increase our giving. In order to receive more, let us give more. The most well known verse of the Bible is John 3:16, where it is shown that God gave us the greatest gift: His son.

"For **God so loved the world** that **he gave his** one and only **Son**, that whoever believes in him shall not perish but have eternal life."

—John 3:16 (NIV)

The amount we have to give is of little concern; what matters most is that we have the heart and pure desire to give.

This is clearly shown in the story of the widow's offering in the Holy Bible in Mark 12:

"Jesus sat down opposite the place where the offerings were put and watched the crowd putting their money into the temple treasury. Many rich people threw in large amounts. But a poor widow came and put in two very small copper coins, worth only a few cents. Calling his disciples to him, Jesus said, 'Truly I tell you, this poor widow has put more into the treasury than all the others. They all gave out of their wealth; but she, out of her poverty, **put in everything**—all she had to live on.'"

—Mark 12:41-44 (NIV)

There is much more than money we can give. The most powerful gift we have is to **allow ourselves to**

be the blessing. Let us bless everyone we come in contact with on our path.

Let us share our talents, prayers, smiles, encouragement, and beautiful words. Let us be there for one another. Jesus gave his prayers and blessings over everyone rather than money. Let us show our love for humanity.

> "Each of you should give
> what you have decided
> in your heart to give,
> not reluctantly or under
> compulsion, for
> **God loves a cheerful giver.**"
> —II Corinthians 9:7 (NIV)

To be cheerful givers, we shall also open our hearts to receive. We can only draw money from a bank account if money has been deposited to begin with. The same is true for our emotional account.

I pray that we all **freely receive and freely give**.

Jesus says in Matthew 13:

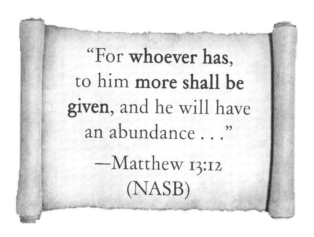

"For **whoever has**,
to him **more shall be
given**, and he will have
an abundance . . ."

—Matthew 13:12
(NASB)

A client came to me and shared her story of how she came to receive—through manifesting—the money to go to a seminar she desired to attend. While at an introductory seminar, she was asked to attend the advanced training. She was short of the required $800 deposit. People at the seminar encouraged her to create the money with her intention, reminding her to focus on already having the money and **leaving the "how" to God**.

Within three weeks, a check for $800 came in the mail for payment of a job that she had completed three years prior when the company put the project on hold. The more astonishing part of the story is that the company asked her to finish the original project and agreed to pay her $3,000 more.

She accepted and they paid her the extra money. The $800 was the exact amount for the seminar deposit and the $3,000 was the exact amount to complete the advanced training! The reason the company chose her to finish the project was because she was the only one who **graciously forgave** them for taking so long to pay. She chose to remain calm during their restructuring time. The final touch on this big studio project took a simple effort of about 10 minutes, because three years prior her team had mostly completed the project.

This story is a beautiful example of a woman cheerfully giving time, effort, and money. She also graciously chose forgiveness while trusting that **God's grace** will take care of her.

"Let us then approach God's throne of grace with **confidence**, so that we may **receive** mercy and find grace to help us in our time of need."

—Hebrew 4:16 (NIV)

"He has saved us and called us to a holy life—not because of anything we have done but because of his own purpose and grace. This **grace was given us** in Christ Jesus before the beginning of time,"

—II Timothy 1:9 (NIV)

"Good will come to those who are **generous and lend freely,** who conduct their affairs with justice."

—Psalm 112:5 (NIV)

Chapter 6

THE EXACTNESS OF
THE UNIVERSE

The Universe has perfect organization and accurate design. Since we are receiving our power from this Source Light Energy, it loves to work with us in exactness. When we are connected with the Source Light Energy, we can **order in extreme detail**. Also, our orders can be multi-dimensional, combining many parameters.

For example, we can add dates, names, places, attitudes, colors, amounts, and desired outcomes. The Universe puts everything in place with beautiful synchronicity. The Universe moves things around in our favor to allow its precise accuracy to be fulfilled to match perfectly with our orders.

Ask And You Shall Receive

We have the opportunity to create with perfect accuracy if we so desire. Allow the Universe to determine "how" it will be done. Still, the exact details are ours to designate as we wish. **Ask and we shall receive**.

All matter exists in neutrality until our mind and words form it. God molds us and we mold our lives. Let us choose to **ask by declaring** our detailed desires with precision using beautiful words.

A client of mine shared his story of creating a car for himself. A black Toyota was his greatest desire. At the time, he was living in Jamaica and owned a barbershop. One February, he was looking at his savings account and it made him realize that the car of his dreams was still just a dream.

He had heard of the Power of Attraction and decided to give it a try. He knew that it was important to **ask for what you desire and leave the "how" open**.

He placed a picture of his dream car on the ceiling over his bed to look at before he went to bed and when he woke up. He visited the car dealership. He sat in the car, started the engine, felt and smelled it, pushed buttons, and turned on the air conditioner. He talked with his friends about the car. He fueled his desire with his excited emotion for the color: "I looove black!" He noticed black cars everywhere he looked. He knew the cost to buy this car was $4,500.

After about a month, he was almost ready to call it quits. He resisted the urge of giving in and continued to believe, remained calm and acted as if he was already the owner of his new car. He actively turned on his inner positive voice that reminded him to stay focused on possessing the car.

"I will have this car for my birthday in May," he told himself. It was March. During the next week, a customer came into his shop noticing that he had extra space available. This customer desired a place for his business and told him the empty area was just what he was looking for. He wished to consult his business partners and contact him later.

My client paid the rent for the whole space, so subleasing the empty portion was a great idea. His customer's business entailed nutrition which complemented his shop. Six weeks later, he finally heard from the customer again. He had almost forgotten about it. A call came from overseas; it was the customer telling him that he was still interested in the space. He wired his rent for an entire year in advance and extra money to have the space cleaned and painted: $2,000 immediately and another $2,000 was promised when the customer returned.

My client was honored by the trust extended to him.

He cleaned up the space and made it ready. When the businessman arrived, he was so pleased with the job that he paid him a $500 bonus. Thus, my client acquired the **exact amount** for his car. He received his dream car in time for his birthday with one small alteration: He decided on a silver one.

A dear friend in my neighborhood **asked** for a biofeedback machine for Christmas. It was two days before Christmas and our Miracle Group met for dinner. At the meeting, she explained that the biofeedback machine was her only Christmas wish.

She wrote down her desire and our Miracle Group encouraged her with our agreement. I asked her how much she wished to pay for the device and why she desired it. She said she was willing to pay $7,000. She asked to have this device in order to help herself, her family, and friends with their health.

The group prayed over her desired gift. Since it was only two days until Christmas, there was little time to order it online. She wished for it to come with a laptop and software already installed, ready for immediate use. A further parameter was that it be available locally for easy pick up. That night, I went out to a business dinner with my husband. The moment I stepped into the restaurant, I bumped into an old friend and the first thing he mentioned to me was that he had his biofeedback machine for sale and inquired if I knew anyone who was interested in buying it. I asked him how much he was selling it for and he replied with the exact number my friend was willing to spend: $7,000.

I said, "SOLD! We will come to your house in the morning and pick it up." The moment I came home, I called to tell my friend that we will be picking up her Christmas gift in the morning. She had been out walking and affirming her excitement of having her gift.

With our **combined precise focus and willful intentions**, her Christmas wish became reality in less than a day.

A businessman sought a bonus that satisfied him for his strategic brilliance. When his wife asked him what amount shall compensate him for his effort, he replied, "$500,000 is my number." His wife wrote down, "My husband is paid a $500,000 bonus this year."

When the bonuses were distributed, his was for $500,000. Out of all possible numbers, the Universe delivered the exact amount he and his wife asked for.

Two sisters were on the phone discussing a charity dinner. One told the other that she was in charge of the ticket sales and coordinating the supplies to match the sales for the event. For the event to be a true success, she and her colleagues desired more sales. She further explained that she had already made great effort to forecast ticket sales and she had arranged for food and resources for a greater number of meals to be served. The charity dinner was being held in two days to benefit her child's school.

Her sister asked, "How many dinners do you wish to sell?" When she hesitated, her sister suggested that she read the number on the package of the paper plates. "144," she replied. Both wrote down in their journals that 144 dinners are sold.

After the event, the final count revealed that exactly 144 dinners were sold that night. God's Universe delivered the very precise, very wonderful, very fantastic miracle of exactly 144 dinner tickets sold.

While my girlfriend and I visited at my house to discuss our future business plans, my husband came in and shared that it was essential for a company he was involved in to receive an additional $10 million in funding.

My husband and I had invested a large amount of money already, so I was motivated to ask for the new money with these parameters: First, our shares hold their value. Second, the money comes from another source other than us personally. Third, the money comes easily with little work for my husband.

My girlfriend and I wrote everything down and seconded the motion. It was a Monday night. By the end of the week, the company received a loan offer in the amount of $10 million with a low interest rate. The money acquired met all my parameters and made my husband and me very happy.

Let us be as specific as possible and **set parameters** when we order, to allow ourselves to receive everything we desire and be joyful.

When our desires are clear and we value our goals enough, we will be specific with our **asking**. When children write a wish list for Santa Claus, it is a very important mission to them. They make their lists as long as possible and are very specific. They know exactly what they are hoping for and what the desired gifts look like.

It is easier to go shopping from a list of desires than to guess what they might be interested in. As parents, we are pleased to see our children's eyes sparkle on Christmas morning. We intend for them to be full of joy for more than one or two days of the year. We aspire to fulfill their desires.

God is our Heavenly Father. He also aspires to

fulfill our desires and delights in our happiness and contentment every day.

One morning, when my daughter was about eight years old, she came into the kitchen and declared to me, "I am asking for $100,000." The evening before, we were on a long walk and I had explained to her that **she can be, have, and do whatever she desires.**

A friend came to visit us and slept in my daughter's bedroom. Shortly after, my friend came out for breakfast. She told my daughter to go to her bedroom and look on top of her pillow, because she had left something there for her.

My daughter ran into her room and came back with a chocolate bar with a picture on the wrapper of a $100,000 bill. She was happy about the gift, although her comment was: "Next time I will **ask for the real thing**!"

One day, when I was driving my old car, a man pulled close and yelled out of the window, "Please sell me your car, lady. I am looking for your exact car."

I wondered to myself why anyone might desire to buy my old car. That night, I went to the YMCA. When I was ready to go home, I turned the key in the ignition and my car was silent. I was stunned, since it was running very well on the way there.

The Exactness Of The Universe

I looked at the odometer; it registered 100,000 miles. I had the car towed to my friend's auto shop and he told me that it was time for a new engine. I searched my mind for what had brought on this incident. I remembered the day I purchased the car from the dealer. On my way home, I thought about how long I intended to keep it. 10 years prior I declared, "I will keep the car for 100,000 miles."

Since we create everything, sometimes we may wish to search our minds to recall when we created it.

Recently, I went shopping at the grocery store only to grab a few things, however, I soon found myself filling the cart. I had some cash in my pocket, although the amount was a secret to me. When I went to check out, I told the cashier that I might require a subtotal, because I only have whatever money is left in my pocket.

With a smile he said, "It will be perfect." I agreed. The total was $81.25. I took the cash from my pocket and handed it to the cashier. It was $81. We both had fun and laughed as the cashier loaned me a quarter.

We are always welcome to change our goals or alter our path at any time. We may change our minds as often as we wish and start **asking** for our new desires. As we focus on what feels good to us in every given moment, it helps us to determine what desires move us toward our goals.

While in the airport waiting for our connecting flight to arrive, my husband and I were informed of our delayed departure due to weather. Since I was flying with someone who prefers other means of transportation, I put on a happy face and let everyone know a little delay was fine with us.

I began to declare that we were patient, happy to wait and our party receiving us on the other end was patient also. Each new announcement brought another delay, and it became apparent that for the flights to remain on schedule, a lot of precision and amazing coordination had to happen. Keeping a positive attitude, I did a lot of praying for everyone involved and waited.

At one point I said, "Enough! Why am I declaring that we are okay with waiting when what I **really desire** is something else? I declare that our plane lands immediately, the passengers disembark quickly, the cleaning crew will prep the plane efficiently and in record time, our flight attendants will be ready to board, and all passengers will start boarding in 10 minutes." In addition to all that, I added, "And we are ready for take-off at 5:15 p.m. with our luggage."

The Exactness Of The Universe

We had waited long enough. My last few texts read:

— 4:57 p.m. from my family, "Are you on the plane yet?"

— 4:58 p.m. from me, "We are still at the gate. I just declared that our plane is boarded and ready to leave for Jacksonville, North Carolina, with our suitcases by 5:15 p.m. today!"

— 5:11 p.m. from me, "In the future I will immediately order what I really wish to create. We are on the plane and ready for departure. See you in an hour."

Our plane was taxiing for take-off at 5:16 p.m. and up in the air exactly according to my newly ordered schedule. It was definitely a God-made miracle!

Chapter 7

THE POWER OF THE WORD

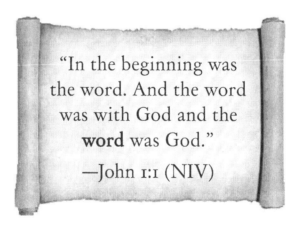

"In the beginning was the word. And the word was with God and the **word** was God."

—John 1:1 (NIV)

Besides forming man, God spoke everything that is into existence. He uses words. **All creation was, is, and will be spoken or written into existence.**

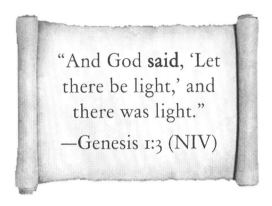

"And God **said**, 'Let there be light,' and there was light."
—Genesis 1:3 (NIV)

God left us *The Holy Bible*. It is a book which, when opened, is full of only one thing: words. The Bible is our manual to this life experience. Every year, it is the number one best-selling book in the world. It supersedes all other book sales by such a great margin, because humankind's powerful and universal desire to know God and His Word is continual.

The word trumps the thought. At a seminar, I had the privilege to walk across hot coals. And even though my mind knew they were hot and my body was questioning my mind, I successfully crossed the coals because of my chanting and anchoring positive words of "Yes, I can. I am walking on cool moss." When my mind questioned the ability of my body to achieve it, my words trumped my mind.

Being a magnetic force, humans attract consciously and subconsciously with the frequencies transmitted from our minds and our hearts. Creation is conscious when we use words.

God was so smart making the word final. Our mind tends to be scattered. Our mind wanders constantly, day and night, in this dimension and others. Everything is created in our conscious state. Our dream state is merely a reflection of our own consciousness. The word performs the final creation. The thought attracts; the word creates.

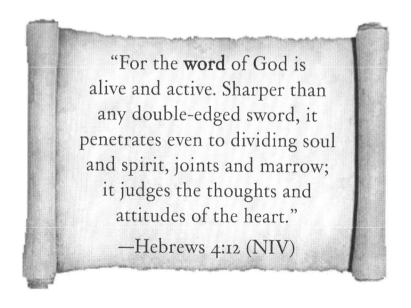

"For the **word** of God is alive and active. Sharper than any double-edged sword, it penetrates even to dividing soul and spirit, joints and marrow; it judges the thoughts and attitudes of the heart."
—Hebrews 4:12 (NIV)

Because we are the children of God, we share His creation power in this Universe. We shall be aware that we have as much power to create the positive as the negative.

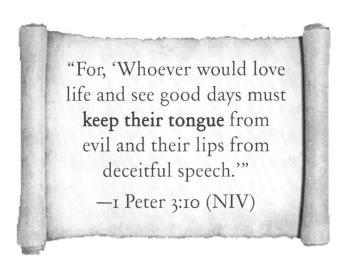

"For, 'Whoever would love life and see good days must **keep their tongue** from evil and their lips from deceitful speech.'"

—1 Peter 3:10 (NIV)

Humans are the only creatures on Earth that are able to speak words. This grants us the unique ability to co-create with God. We are His greatest creation and we are made in His image. Because He creates, we can create, and He creates by speaking things into existence.

Like Him, we create with the use of our words. Let us be conscious of our use of words. Let us extend our vocabulary to say what we really mean in order to always create what is good.

Words are symbols whose meanings people have agreed on. God told Adam to name every animal on

Earth. He has the ability to name everything Himself and yet He has the desire to interact and co-create with us. Right from the beginning, God chose man to co-create with Him and encouraged us to use our words to do it.

"Now the LORD God had formed out of the ground all the wild animals and all the birds in the sky. He brought them to the man to see what he would **name** them; and whatever the man called each living creature, that was its name. So the **man gave names to all** the livestock, the birds in the sky and all the wild animals. . . ."

—Genesis 2:19-20 (KJV)

The agreements about the meanings we have for every single word we use prompt thoughts, images, and stories in our minds. A thought takes us one place at a time; a word can set a whole movie full of many connected thoughts in motion. Every word sparks a unique memory for everyone. Compound words generate a different image or movie in our mind than a single word.

Think about the word "God." We may think about His creation power, our relationship with Him or our favorite Bible verse. Next, let us think about "Father." We may picture God or our biological father with a whole flood of memories. Now, let us visualize "Godfather." Most likely, a person dear to us pops into our head or possibly an entire movie. Combined words hold a different creation power than a single word. One of my favorite exercises to show this phenomenon came from a writing class in which the teacher wrote a random word on the board and we were to write our memory about it in one minute. He chose common words like "hair" and "bread." Everyone came up with brilliant stories from years gone by. Each word activates a memory. Every story for every word is unique for everyone, as are the pictures in our mind and our agreements of each meaning.

> *Try this out!*
>
> *Think of the word "Cinderella."*
>
> *What does it evoke in your mind?*
>
> _____
>
> _____
>
> _____
>
> _____

We may think about when someone read the story to us at bedtime or when we watched the famous Disney movie. We may even identify with one of the characters. Are we the princess or prince living happily ever after? Are we identifying with the stepmother or one of the mice? A friend of mine definitely identifies with the fairy godmother; this is what she is for my children. The association my sister holds with this story and other fairytales is that the mother always dies. The concept I took from the movie was, "Whomever the shoe fits." What I mean by this is: I look for the shoe that fits my foot.

The Power Of The Word

There are also words with a variety of meanings. For example, the word "shalom" is so complex and beautiful that it holds the meaning of peace, harmony, wholeness, completeness, prosperity, welfare, tranquility, hello, and goodbye. "Namaste" contains the understanding of I bow to the divine in you.

Growing up, we simply accept word definitions we are taught. Then, along the way, we form our own meanings through our own experiences. Our belief system is formed. We all come from different backgrounds, which leads to varied beliefs and understanding of words. These different realities are articulated especially in our relationships with our loved ones. So clarification about what we really mean is advisable when we speak with others as their understanding might differ from ours.

The creation power comes with the tongue. With the use of our words we influence all matter, including ourselves and even water.

Chapter 8

THE POWER OF IMPRINTING
WATER WITH WORDS

Vibration is the force that moves us. Everything in existence vibrates. Our words vibrate, creating resonance, which forms energy. Words themselves are energy. Energy is vibration and vibrations form life, light, and sound. Therefore, words are life!

These vibrations have an immediate impact on the physical. Our world is constantly changing and water is the first to recognize change. Water registers and reflects any frequency it is exposed to.

Masaru Emoto, Ph.D. spent his life researching and educating humanity about water's true nature and the effect our words and all vibrations have on water. His incredible water crystal photography demonstrates to our amazement how our thoughts, words, emotions, prayers, and music are truly vibrations that actually change the structure of water.

Emoto's legacy involved freezing water samples, after they have been exposed to various vibrational frequencies, to see if they formed into beautiful crystals or showed the absence of molecular structure almost resembling mud. When a vial of water had a beautiful word such as "love," "gratitude," "happiness," or "thank you" labeled on it, according to Dr. Emoto's tests the water in the vial froze into perfect beautiful snowflakes with every word forming a unique crystal. The language the word was written in on the vial was irrelevant. Continually, the positive words froze with beautiful crystal structure and the negative words froze without structure. He proved to the world that positive words hold creation power and are in tune with nature; negative words lack creation power.

Here is a list of words and phrases that formed beautiful water crystals:

adoration	faith
affection	family love
amen	friend
angel	happiness
beautiful	Happy Christmas
Buddhism	harmony
change	heart
Christianity	home cooking
clasping hands	honesty
compassion	hope
courtesy	I can do it
Dad	I love you
dream	imagine
dreams come true	innocence
emotion	it's going to be all right
energetic	Jehovah
enjoyment	Judaism
eternal	let's do it
eternity	love and gratitude
everything is going to	love and thanks
work out	love of country
exhilaration	Love of humanity

love of husband and wife	thanks to you
Mom	the reason for living
namaste	to feel
neighborly love	truth
patriotism	unification
peace	we are all water
peace of mind	wedded Love
resonance	well done
reverence	wisdom
self love	you are beautiful
spousal love	you are pretty
star	you did well
star of David	you tried hard
thank you (in different languages)	and so on

Thus, I encourage myself and all humanity to add these words and phrases to our vocabulary.

Ask And You Shall Receive

Here is a list of words, phrases and waves that showed absence of form when frozen:

blasphemy	*human cloning*
convenience food	*I can't do it*
despair	*ignore*
devil	*isolate*
dislike	*it's hopeless*
do it	*must*
the electromagnetic	*rage and murder*
field of telephone,	*that's no good*
television,	*ugly*
computer, and	*unhappiness*
microwave oven	*war*
exhaustion	*you are stupid*
fool	*you fool*
foolish	and so on
hate	

Thus, I encourage myself and all humanity to omit these words and phrases from our vocabulary.

We live on a planet covered with water. Just as in our human body, 70 percent is made up of water. Water is life.

In the beginning of the Bible, the **Holy Spirit** and the **water** already existed:

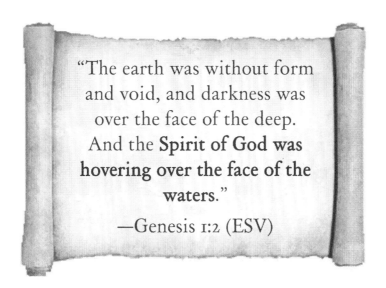

"The earth was without form and void, and darkness was over the face of the deep. And the **Spirit of God was hovering over the face of the waters.**"

—Genesis 1:2 (ESV)

The power of our beautiful words, thoughts, and prayers can be used to purify water. In a water study, one photograph was taken before an incantation of love and beauty, and another was taken after the prayer. The second photograph showed a fantastic difference—the water was remarkably clearer.

Every word holds the energy of the **Holy Spirit**. The power of the prayer came from the Spirit of the spoken word. Is it possible that this energy of the Holy Spirit purified the water in the lake? It was marvelous; the water became more and more transparent as they looked at it. The vibrations of words are affecting objects, people, and water in an immediate way.

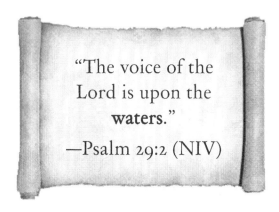

"The voice of the Lord is upon the **waters**."
—Psalm 29:2 (NIV)

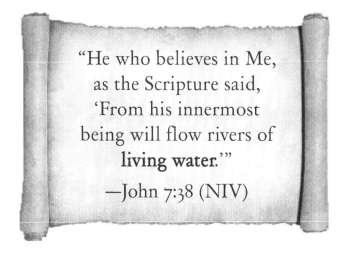

"He who believes in Me, as the Scripture said, 'From his innermost being will flow rivers of **living water**.'"
—John 7:38 (NIV)

We are made of mostly water. We are born in water. Water is necessary to sustain life. Many stories in the Bible depict miraculous happenings around water.

In the beginning, God separated the land from the water.

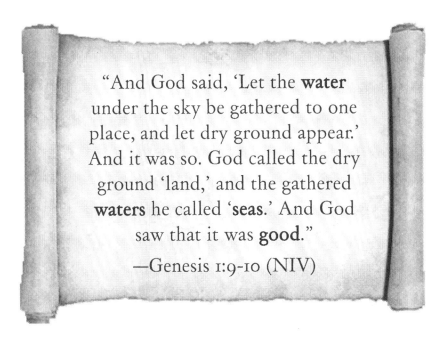

"And God said, 'Let the **water** under the sky be gathered to one place, and let dry ground appear.' And it was so. God called the dry ground 'land,' and the gathered **waters** he called 'seas.' And God saw that it was **good**."

—Genesis 1:9-10 (NIV)

When Moses struck the rod on the rock out came **water** (Numbers 20:11). God parted the **Red Sea** for the Israelites to cross (Exodus 14). We baptize with **water**. Jesus was baptized in the **water** of the **Jordan River** (Matthew 3:13). Jesus first recorded miracle was turning **water** into wine (John 2:1-12). Peter walked on the **water** (Matthew 14:29). In Noah's time, the **Great Flood** cleansed the Earth with **water**. (Genesis 6:9-9:17). Water is a theme throughout the Bible.

Ask And You Shall Receive

Since Dr. Emoto has made us aware that water is imprintable with beautiful words, let us take the time to speak kind words over our water before we drink it.

We can label our glasses, glass water bottles, as well as our pitchers, with beautiful words. Then our water is blessed with our words and the blessings are poured into our body throughout the day. In addition, we can label our water with everything we wish for, for example:

- ♥ I am in perfect health.

- ♥ My life is full of happiness.

- ♥ I am a genius.

- ♥ Money flows frequently and abundantly to me.

- ♥ I have the power to control and direct my own mind.

- ♥ I have God's wisdom. I make wise decisions.

Beyond the imprinted effects, reading the affirmations and inspirations throughout the day anchors them into our minds.

The Power Of Imprinting Water With Words

God spoke over his church body and blessed it:

"to make her holy,
cleansing her by the
washing with **water
through the word**,"
—Ephesians 5:26 (NIV)

"for an angel of the Lord went
down at certain seasons into the
pool and **stirred up the water**;
whoever then first, after the stirring
up of the **water**, stepped in was
made well from whatever disease
with which he was afflicted."
—John 5:4 (NIV)

The angel's vibration over the water created a reaction influencing the molecular structure of the water.

Humans are as imprintable as water. It does matter which words we use to talk to ourselves and other beings. Every word matters. Matter changes to match our words. Jesus changed matter and healed with his words:

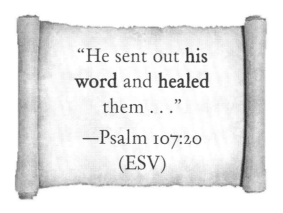

"He sent out **his word** and **healed** them . . ."

—Psalm 107:20 (ESV)

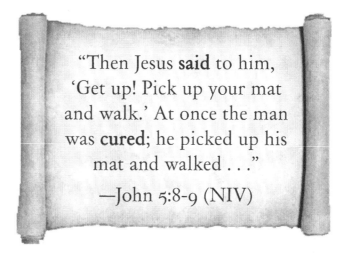

"Then Jesus **said** to him, 'Get up! Pick up your mat and walk.' At once the man was **cured**; he picked up his mat and walked . . ."

—John 5:8-9 (NIV)

"The centurion replied,
'Lord, I do not deserve to
have you come under my
roof. But **just say the word**,
and my servant will be
healed.'"
—Matthew 8:8 (NIV)

"Then the father realized that
this was the exact time at
which Jesus had **said** to him,
'Your son **will live**.'
So he and his whole
household believed."
—John 4:53 (NIV)

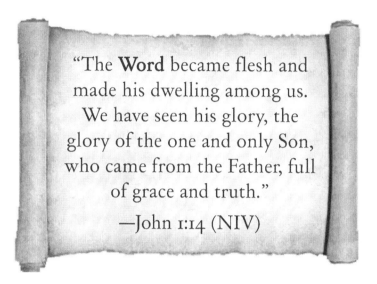

"The **Word** became flesh and made his dwelling among us. We have seen his glory, the glory of the one and only Son, who came from the Father, full of grace and truth."
—John 1:14 (NIV)

Let us rediscover the truth of the Word.

Chapter 9

THE POWER OF USING POSITIVE WORDS AS A BLESSING

Every word is a creation. We can choose to create love, joy, gratitude, hope, compassion, mercy, praise, and much more positivity with our words—or we can choose to create the lack thereof.

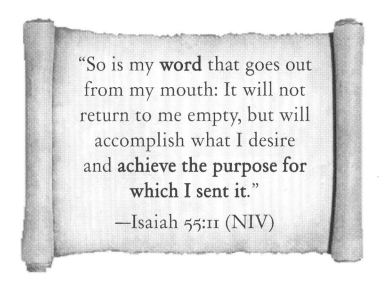

"So is my **word** that goes out from my mouth: It will not return to me empty, but will accomplish what I desire and **achieve the purpose for which I sent it.**"

—Isaiah 55:11 (NIV)

Are our words supporting our purpose? Let us be conscious of which words we send out to achieve what we desire.

One of my favorite neighbors volunteered to co-chair a local charity event. Besides being asked to raise money, solicit sponsorships, and create collateral for the event, she was also assigned the task of collecting donations for a grand "winner-takes-all" raffle drawing.

Over a period of eight months, she put her heart and soul into the project and personally collected more than $28,000 in gift certificates, services, and merchandise ranging from a year of hair cuts at a local salon, a six-hour appointment with a professional organizer, and a diamond necklace to a deluxe massage package and a complete car detailing for the drawing.

Two days before the event, I went over to see how things were coming along and noticed that the gift baskets, bags, and boxes, previously contained to the guest room, had surprisingly taken over her entire condominium.

When I pointed this out, my friend said, "In two days, it will all be gone and out of my home, and all I can say is; it better *not* come back."

I was cognizant of her power of her words and,

sure enough, a few days later, I saw all of the baskets, bags, and boxes piled up in the middle of her living room.

As it turns out, her mother, who had attended the event as her guest, had purchased nine raffle tickets and won the entire lot. In a state of shock, my friend and her mother loaded up their cars and brought everything back home to be sorted out and inventoried, divvied up, and donated, all over again, to five very appreciative local charities.

This truly was the gift that kept on giving. What she really meant to say was, "I am ready once again to enjoy my clean house" or "I am excited to have my house and space to myself again."

Let us speak clearly of what we invite in our lives. The Universe chooses to focus and reacts to words with creation ability to provide what we are asking for. It sorts, processes and eliminates other words. Our word choice might confuse the meaning of what we are trying to accomplish and may cause a reaction taking us in the complete opposite direction from our goal.

> "Not what goes into the mouth defiles a man; but **what comes out of the mouth**, this defiles a man."
>
> —Matthew 15:11 (NKJV)

When my 91-year-old friend and yoga instructor was ready to live in a nursing home, we went through all his important documents. He chose me to be executor of his will. I talked with him about his long-term insurance policy and asked him to tell me the story of when he bought it.

His words were, "The sales person told me that I will most likely never use it, but it is good to have anyway." He bought the policy and paid the annual premiums for 35 years, which amounted to roughly $350,000. The policy stated that in the case that the policyholder moves to a nursing home, the first 60 days rent will be paid by the policyholder before the insurance begins coverage. My friend passed on after 59 days in the nursing home.

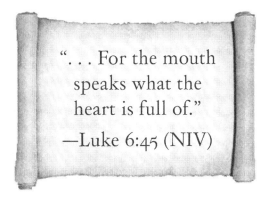

"... For the mouth speaks what the heart is full of."

—Luke 6:45 (NIV)

Are our words defining us? Are we conscious and aware of our own words? Do we understand the power of our own words? Are we encouraging ourselves and others with every word we speak?

Words come from organized thoughts so it is important to write down our words for organization. A study by Dr. Matthias Mehl and his team at the University of Arizona found that women and men speak an average of 16,000 words per day. The Laboratory of Neuro Imaging estimates an average person has roughly 70,000 thoughts per day.

Monitoring thoughts takes time, rightmindedness, extreme concentration, and consciousness. Editing words is more doable. Since our words come from our thoughts, if we simply listen to our own words, we can tell how positive our thoughts are in every moment.

Positive thoughts become positive words. If our use of positive words requires further development, this may show that our thoughts yearn for conscious enhancement.

In the beginning was the Word. We can start by rediscovering all the good words and train our minds to use expanded positive vocabulary. Let us always speak kind words of abundance. To some of us it might feel like learning a new language. This new language is conscious creation.

From today forward, please actively use this list of beautiful words to enhance your current vocabulary. These are words I collected. I hope they inspire you to write your own list or add to mine.

BEAUTIFUL WORD LIST

A
abundant
accomplished
achieving
active
admirable
admired
adorable
advanced
adventure
adventurous
affection
affirmations
affluent
agreeable
aligned
alive
already
always
amazing
amen
angelic
appealing

appreciation
artistic
astonishing
astounding
astute
attentive
attractive
auspicious
authentic
awake
aware
awe
awesome

_____

_____

_____

B
beaming
beautiful
beauty
believe

beneficial
benefit
best
better all the time
bless
blessings
bliss
bold
brave
breathtaking
bright
brilliant
buoyant

_____

_____

_____

C
calm
capable
caring
celebrate
centered
certain

change
charming
cheerful
child-like
choice
clarity
clear
clever
closeness
colorful
comfortable
commitment
communion
companionship
compassion
competent
complete
confident
congratulations
connected
conscious
considerate
content
courageous
courtesy

The Power Of Using Positive Words

creative
cute

_____

_____

D
dancing
daring
dazzling
declare
delicious
delightful
depth
desirable
determined
devoted
diligent
discerning
distinguished
divine
divine love
dominate
dream

dynamic

_____

_____

_____

E
eagerness
easy
ecstatic
effective
efficient
elated
elegant
eloquent
emotion
empowerment
energetic
energy
enjoyment
enthusiasm
enticing
essential
eternal
eternity

everlasting
evolving
excellent
exceptional
exciting
exhale
experienced
exquisite
exuberant

_____

_____

_____

F
fabulous
fair
faith
family love
famous
fantastic
fascinating
favorable
fine
finish
flattering

flourishing
flowing
focused
forevermore
forgive
fortunate
forward
free
freedom
friendly
fruitful
fulfilled
fun

_____

_____

_____

G
generous
genius
gentle
genuine
gift
gifted
give thanks

gleaming
glee
glorious
glory
glowing
goals
good
good-looking
goodness
gorgeous
grace
graceful
gracious
grand
gratitude
great
greatness
growing
growth

_____

_____

_____

H
handsome
happiness

happy
harmonious
harmony
healed
healthy
heart
heartwarming
heaven
helpful
honesty
honored
hope
hopeful
hug
humorous

_____

_____

_____

I
I am
ideal
imaginative
imagine
impressive
in tune

increase
incredible
industrious
ingenious
innocence
innovative
inspiration
instantaneously
intelligent
interesting
intimacy
intuitive
inventive
invigorate
inviting

_____

_____

_____

J
Jesus
joy
jubilant

_____

_____

_____

K
keen
kindness
knowing

_____

_____

_____

L
laugh
lead
let us
life-giving
light
lightness
likable
lively
love
lovely
loving
luminous

_____

_____

_____

M
magical
magnificent
marvelous
masterful
meaningful
mercy
merit
mighty
mindful
miraculous
more
motivated
music

_____

_____

_____

N
natural
neat
new
nice
noble
now

nurturing
nutritious

_____

_____

_____

O
one
open
optimism
optimistic
outstanding

_____

_____

_____

P
passionate
patience
peace
peaceful
perfect
persevering
persistent

phenomenal
playful
pleasing
pleasure
plentiful
popular
positive
possible
power
powerful
prayer
precious
prefer
prepared
presence
pretty
productive
profound
progress
prominent
prompt
prosperous
proud
pure
purify

_____

_____

_____

Q
quality
quick
quiet

_____

_____

R
radiance
ready
receive
rediscover
refined
refreshing
regard
reimagine
rejoice
rejuvenate
relationship
relaxing

reliable
remarkable
renewal
renewing
resolute
resonance
resourceful
respectful
restored
reverence
rewarding
rich
right

_____

_____

_____

S
satisfied
self love
self-reliant
sensational
sensible
sensitive
serene
serenity

shalom
sharing
simple
skillful
smart
smile
smooth
soulful
sparkling
special
spirit
spiritual
splendid
spontaneity
strength
strong
stunning
successful
sunny
superb
supporting
surprising

_____

_____

_____

T
talented
terrific
thankful
thriving
transform
true
trust
truth
truthful

_____

_____

_____

U
understanding
unification
unique

_____

_____

_____

_____

V
valuable
versatile
vibrant
vibrations
victorious
vital
vivacious

_____

_____

_____

W
warm
water
wealthy
welcome
well
well being
well done
whole
wisdom
wise

wonderful   Z
words   zeal
world   zest
world peace
worthy
wow

_____   _____

_____   _____

_____   _____

Jesus says in Revelation:

"**Coming out of his mouth is a sharp sword** with which to strike down the nations. He will rule them with an iron scepter."

—Revelation 19:15 (NIV)

That tells us that when He comes back, He will bring only one thing: His tongue to clean up the world with His Word. In the Holy Bible, Paul reminds us:

"Let your **conversation** be **gracious** and **attractive** so that you will have the right response for everyone."
—Colossians 4:6 (NLT)

Let us always be consciously aware of our words. Let us train to clean up our words. Let us **edit ourselves constantly**. Life is a masterpiece of continual creation.

As we write through our lives, let us be eager to make improvements by checking the words we choose to **ask** and create with. Are all the words we use uplifting and full of light? Remember, what radiates out of us comes back to us.

Let us always be clear about **why** we desire to have, do, and achieve everything. For example, before we go into a meeting or call anyone, let us be sure to write down the exact desired outcome to be achieved in this moment.

> I am calling (texting, emailing, having lunch with, ...)
> _____ (name) with
> the desire to _____
> (goal) because I _____
> _____ (state reason why)."

Add details and define why we desire for something to transpire. Knowing why we desire something creates emotional connection to the outcome and increases the Power of Attraction. Feel wonderful about asking for it, declaring it will occur, and calling it in. Be happy and excited to receive the new creation.

Whenever we wish to create anything, let us write it down, read it, revisit it, and **edit ourselves three times**. Make sure that:

- ♥ Everything is stated in the positive

- ♥ Our words are uplifting

- ♥ Our focus is clear and determined

♥ Everything is written in the present tense as
  if it is happening or has already happened
  and is here now

♥ Articulate why you desire to have it

Remember, the Universe *"needs and wants for
nothing"*. God's Universe already has and contains
everything. If you are *"going to get"* something or
"want" something, the Quantum Field allows us to
"keep going and going" and *"wanting and wanting"* and
"trying to get." Let us move on from the *"wanting state"*
and declare that all is already here.

When Moses said to God in Exodus 3:13,

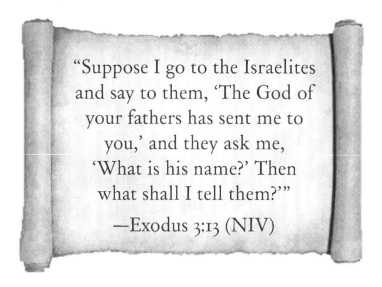

"Suppose I go to the Israelites
and say to them, 'The God of
your fathers has sent me to
you,' and they ask me,
'What is his name?' Then
what shall I tell them?'"

—Exodus 3:13 (NIV)

God answered in Exodus 3:14,

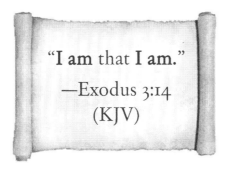

"I am that I am."
—Exodus 3:14
(KJV)

Human vocabulary is too confined to describe God, thus His title remains wide open with all possibilities when He said, "I AM that I AM." He is a true Quantum Being. He is the great "I AM" of all. In Hebrew, "I am" can be translated as He who is, was, and will always be.

God spoke **I am** that **I am**. Let us stay in flow with His Creation Power and choose to start our list of desires ("Miracle List") the same way. Let us also add the positive spirit of gratitude to be present in us throughout the day. Let us write our lists of what we truly request using the words:

"I am grateful that I am (I have)

_____

_____

_____

_____

_____

_____

_____"

The Power Of Using Positive Words

Here are a few examples:

- ♥ **I am** grateful that **I am** in perfect health.

- ♥ **I am** grateful that **I am** fulfilled and have a fantastic relationship with my loving spouse.

- ♥ **I am** grateful that **I am** the owner of a new white truck with a powerful engine and large wheels that easily pulls my jet skis to the ocean.

The more details we write down, the more completely our mind focuses on our order. Also, it becomes more clear to us and the Universe. Whenever we place our order for this very moment, we can **add "and more"** to leave it open to the Universe to happily surprise us with additional blessings.

When my friend was backing down the driveway, her son told her, "Mom, you are a *bad* driver." She replied, "Have I ever involved us in an accident?" While saying this, she backed into a tree.

Let us practice re-stating our order by re-declaring what we prefer immediately: "**What I really mean is** . . ." or "**I prefer** . . ." Let us practice our positive words and use them always with all the people around us.

Ask And You Shall Receive

A few years ago, my children gave me a plaque for Christmas with a common saying on it: "*Don't worry about tomorrow, God is already there.*" The first thing I did was place a new phrase over the first two words: "Be inspired."

It sat on my desk for over a month before I realized two more necessary corrections. We live in a series of **present moments** and we ask our God to be **here** with us **today**. With this change, the plaque now declares: "**Be inspired** about **today**, God is already **here**."

If our words have the power to bless or the opposite, let us decide to make every word count. This entails bringing the common phrases we use all the time to our awareness, allowing us to change every word to a blessing. Let us convert them into positive creations. Let us be conscious of what we are calling in with our exact words in every moment.

For example, when we say that we will "*unleash* our power," it suggests to the Universe that it has to create a "leash" in order to fulfill our thought or command to be "*unleashed.*" Similarly, "*unstoppable*" suggests one may currently be "*stopped*" and if by chance we are flowing, the Universe now has an order to "*stop*" us in order to free us from the stop. This theory reveals that we spend a lot of time creating things to "*un*"-create.

It lacks efficiency, uses double the effort, and

creates a confusing order. This is like running away from the finish line when our original intention is to run toward it.

To be a "*warrior* for peace," the Universe will help to find a "*battle*." "The sky is the *limit*." Is the sky *limited*? Having "*unlimited* power" suggests a limit as well. Two phrases used too often are "*don't worry*" and "*no worries*." Why do we desire to create "*worry*" in order "*not to*"? When God created in the first page of the Bible, he said all is "**good**." How brilliant! We humans tend to say "*not bad*," when what we really mean is the opposite. God uses proper words to say what He means. Let us follow in His image.

We use these sayings even though they lack efficiency. The results we call in may be the opposite of what we desire to call in.

Below is a list of commonly used phrases to become aware of and conscious options to possibly be used instead.

Lack of consciousness	Conscious choices
at *least*	I am so happy that
debt free	financially sound, abundant
don't *forget*	remember
don't *worry*	be happy
effortless	easy
fight, battle	do your best
fixed income	ever increasing income
I *can't* wait	I am ready
I *don't blame* you	I agree
if it is *not* this, then it is something else	life just becomes better, God is good
in*finite*	continual

Lack of consciousness	Conscious choices
it will *not* be *difficult*	it is easy
must	let us
never-ending, endless	continual
no doubt	absolutely, with certainty, for sure
no problem, not a *problem*	you are welcome, blessings
no *worries*	you are welcome, blessings
not a *bad* idea	it is a good idea, brilliant
not bad	good
nothing is *lost*	it is all here
nothing is *wrong* with it	it's all right
out*rage*ous	fun, out of the ordinary

Lack of consciousness	Conscious choices
pain free, *pain less, no pain*	feel great, perfect health
sick	returning to perfect health
stop smoking	perfect (lung) health
stress-free, *less stress*	easy, calm, relaxed
terribly beautiful	very beautiful
that's *not* so *dumb*	that's genius
there is *nothing* in my life I *can't* do	I can achieve everything
*un*believable	it is believable
unconditional love	perfect love
undone	put together
unleash	free flowing, allow
*unlimit*ed power	perfect power

Lack of consciousness	Conscious choices
unstoppable	continuing
want	choose, prefer, desire, seek
*war*rior	Light being (Jesus, the Prince of Peace)
what else can *go wrong*	everything is going all right
you *can't* miss it	you will definitely see it
you *won't* believe this	you will believe this
why *don't* we	let us

Carefully listen to the words we use and the words everyone around us uses. Start practicing alternate positive words until they become a new, wonderful habit. Please encourage us by adding your empowering conscious word choices to this list by sending an email to: ask@receivejoy.com

"Let no corrupting **talk come out of your mouths**, but only such as is **good** for building up, as fits the occasion, that it may give grace to those who hear."
—Ephesians 4:29 (ESV)

"I tell you, on the day of judgment people will give account for every careless **word** they speak,"
—Matthew 12:36 (ESV)

This is why Mother Theresa said, "If you invite me to an *anti-war* rally, I will pass. But if you invite me to a peace gathering, I will be there."

The Power Of Using Positive Words

If anyone hands us words that lack blessing, respond with blessed uplifting words. For example, "Yes, may God continue to bless me and you!" or "Have a nice day!"

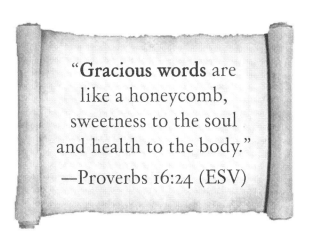

"**Gracious words** are
like a honeycomb,
sweetness to the soul
and health to the body."
—Proverbs 16:24 (ESV)

Let us also be conscious of only sharing our happy stories. Please refrain from telling the other stories. Every time a story is retold, we are recreating it all over again and drawing it into the present, thus adding fuel to negativity. We are assisting in attracting more of it. In other words, the negative fire is kindled.

Once an elderly gentleman came to my house and told me about his car accident from years ago. He offered to show me pictures of him injured. I invited him to show me pictures of all the good things in his life and explained to him that this will bring me greater joy.

Ask And You Shall Receive

Let us share our happy stories as well as our dreams and desires. We will still have plenty to talk about.

Our words create everything. Every word counts.

When I was growing up, my parents often said to me "*don't* put every word on the golden scale" whenever I questioned their silly words. My inner being knew that every word counts.

Now I understand what they really meant by using this saying. I learned to remain neutral to silly phrases, although now I comprehend that the whole Universe literally weighs every word. I am thankful that they gave me a questioning awareness of the Power of the Word.

When we joke with our words, awareness is also necessary as our words are always in creation mode. The author of this book chooses to speak only beautiful truth—or use duct tape.

"Do you see a man who is **hasty in his words**? There is more hope for a fool than for him."

—Proverbs 29:20 (ESV)

"The **soothing tongue** is a tree of life, but a perverse tongue crushes the spirit."

—Proverbs 15:4 (NIV)

Chapter 10

THE POWER OF EMOTION

The Universe is supernaturally created and designed to deliver our creations. This delivery system is a magnificent, allowing, and flowing force. It is free of emotion. It just exists. It is the same yesterday, today, tomorrow, and forever. It just is.

God created and we create our lives. We are the co-authors and co-creators of our lives. We are co-creators. God Himself has emotions and because we are of God, we have His emotional power.

Emotions are available to enhance our creations. Although we always have the choice to remain neutral, emotions help us to increase the speed of our creation and keep the focus on our intention behind our desires. Emotions influence our thoughts. Our creative words can further be propelled by emotions. Emotions are the driving force behind the word.

According to "The Map of Consciousness" created by David R. Hawkins, M.D., Ph.D., different emotions carry different frequencies. Positive emotions oscillate at higher frequencies.

Enlightenment vibrates at over 700 Hz, Peace resonates at around 600 Hz, Joy 540 Hz, Love 528 Hz, Acceptance 350 Hz, and Neutrality 250 Hz whereas *Anger* holds a lower vibration of around 150 Hz, *Fear* 100 Hz, *Grief* 75 Hz, *Guilt* 30 Hz, and *Shame* 20 Hz.

Thus, when we vibrate with peace, love, and joy, we are a stronger magnetic force. Every time we choose a positive emotion, we instantly match the vibrational field of the Universe. We can consciously feel good by design and feel good all the time. When we stand up tall, confident, and have a smile, we can match the physical expression of our bodies to our beautiful desires.

If we desire greatness, let us feel greatness and exude greatness. Feel it, live it, walk it, love it.

Again, we may choose to remain neutral, as there is peaceful power in neutrality. It is the state of calm well-being. It is our reset vibration. We feel all is well when we are neutral.

Our body communicates with us through feelings. Our feelings are lived out through our emotions. Emotions are our feelings made manifest. Feelings stimulate our emotional state. Thus, our **gut feeling is our gauge** that allows us to be aware whether we seek to move toward something or away from it.

Our gut feelings are a gift. They allow us sensitivity to what we are experiencing. We can use two simple phrases to describe our major gut feelings: either something feels good and we welcome more of it and move toward it or we feel the opposite—when change is required—so we move away from it. Another way to put it is, "This is my blessing" or "This is someone else's blessing."

On the way to the Florida Keys, a businessman took his wife, three teenage daughters, niece, and nephew deep sea fishing. Like a seasoned fisherman, he found it a great blessing to be out at sea and feel the boat rolling in the waves. Instead of sitting in his office all day, he enjoyed being out fishing.

What he wished to be a perfect family outing turned out to be a lesser blessing for half of his family. The smell of dead fish and motion sickness overcame the girls. While for some people fishing is what they dream of doing for pleasure, others may prefer to enjoy fish underwater while scuba diving.

The Power Of Emotion

When we are comparing people, places, and things, it is often best to say what we prefer and leave it at that. Refrain from commenting on the opposite of our preference. Let us bless whatever we like and allow in whatever feels right. Let us feel free to exercise our right to let anything pass that we prefer less of. Grant it to another, as it may be their blessing. We all have very unique desires.

Chapter 11

THE POWER OF OUR INNER GUIDANCE SYSTEM

Let us choose to make this our life of joy. I can have, be, and attract everything I choose. When we have faith and choose to live in joy, our clear, specific perspective appears. The true splendor of the power, from Whom we came, is revealed. This Universe is full of total possibilities.

Man is often looking outside himself for the truth when, in fact, the **perfect guidance system is within**. First, let us learn to listen to our inner self. Accessing the real truth can only come from within.

Our gut feelings are our inner guidance system. This gut feeling expresses itself in one of two ways:

It makes us feel good and compels us to move toward it, or the opposite, when we choose to move away from it. Let us choose to feel good right now. Let us choose to feel better and better all the time.

When I was a student in Germany, my university had three partner universities abroad with nine scholarship positions. My dream was always to study abroad, and three spots were open at Michigan State University, one spot at Judson University in Illinois, and five spots in India.

I was doing well academically; yet others were doing better. Overhearing lots of conversations in the hallways, I realized almost everyone was eager to apply for the study abroad program. I thought going to India held the highest probability and so I was preparing myself mentally to go to India when I filled out my application.

One evening, before the application due date, I had a **gut feeling directing me to be completely honest with myself**. I said to myself that I deserve to follow my heart and do what feels right and best for me. I sat down and changed my whole application and applied to go to a university in the United States of America instead. I felt very confident about my application.

The next few days were very exciting; I expected to receive a call to be interviewed for my spot at any time.

I knew from previous years that my university usually asks the students why they considered themselves to be good candidates to be selected.

However, my phone was quiet. Later, when I saw everyone standing in front of the bulletin board, I was pretty sure I had missed my chance. A great number of students were in the hallway, blocking my view to the bulletin board, when one of my classmates turned around and said, "Congratulations! They picked you." I was the only student chosen to attend Judson, a Christian university.

Growing up in East Germany, I prayed for myself and perhaps attended church three times with my grandmother. Although I lived without a Bible, I had the inner knowledge that God exists. I always knew that He loves me, and He desires to give me whatever I desire. He sent me to fill the only spot at the Christian university.

Further, He gave me the opportunity to do an internship in Florida before starting university in Illinois. Because of this, I now had my own Bible and all the English vocabulary I required to study in the United States. During my internship, I spent my first paycheck on scuba diving lessons, because I always dreamt of seeing sharks underwater. Best of all, the seed of truth was planted.

This all came true once I followed my gut feeling

and started to be absolutely honest with myself as to what I really desire.

Let us decide to fill out the applications that gain complete fulfillment for us and pass by the applications that hold only safe probability. Again, the Universe will deliver what we ask for. Ask for your highest aspiration!

Chapter 12

THE POWER OF STARTING NEW

We are currently here now. We came to this very moment through all the experiences and decisions we have made in our creation and called in up to this point. Welcome it all in with acceptance. **Everything is perfect as it is right now**.

Let us experience the perfection of the moment, even if the perfection is presently hiding from our view. Focus on the beauty of the situation. Whatever yesterday felt like, let it go and move ahead with confidence.

Start each day fresh. **We are new every day**. Enrich and embrace every moment with our positive thoughts, beautiful words, and renewed presence.

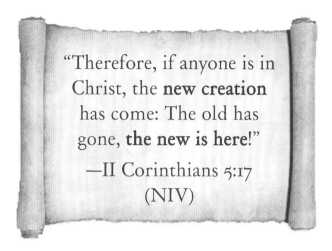

"Therefore, if anyone is in Christ, the **new creation** has come: The old has gone, **the new is here!**"
—II Corinthians 5:17 (NIV)

A few years back, my friend felt she was at odds with her neighbor. There was a point at which her neighbor informed her, "Be careful—your cat might disappear." She responded by putting up a big fence around her back yard.

Years later, she wrote down in her journal, "I view my world friendly and everyone loves me as much as I love myself." She started to radiate love and acceptance toward all. Soon after, her neighbor changed. From then on, he helped her. After laying pavers in her driveway, he even laid a sidewalk along her house leading to the backyard for free.

We control everything with our mind. Forgiveness is a conscious, deliberate decision process releasing feelings. It is our choice to vibrate with forgiveness.

Love is freely and continually forgiving. God shows total forgiveness.

Let us strive to be **forever giving**. Let us forgive ourselves. Let us free ourselves of all extra baggage. Let us give ourselves permission to be.

"Bear with each other and **forgive** one another if any of you has a grievance against someone. **Forgive as the Lord forgave you.**"

—Colossians 3:13 (NIV)

Let us constantly choose to let the past be just that and let each new moment be our NOW—a new experience full of possibilities. Every day is new. **We are new every moment.** We start every day in total forgiveness and with a clean white tablecloth.

"Neither do people pour new wine into old wineskins. If they do, the skins will burst; the wine will run out and the wineskins will be ruined. No, they pour new wine into new wineskins, and both are preserved."

—Matthew 9:17 (NIV)

We are new wineskins when we allow God's light to flow through us. For this to be possible, we first shall allow all humanity to be exactly who they are.

Each of us is a happy and whole being filled with God's love and light. We choose to see the perfection in ourselves and everyone else just as we are in this very moment. Let us bring our focus inside ourselves at all times, because all the answers are already within. Let us be a new wineskin, so that God can fill us and we can shine His light.

This can happen when we are happily conscious of our thoughts, words, and deeds. Let our minds be open, calm, and relaxed. He desires us to be a new wineskin and be ready and willing to accept the new wine that He offers. Our new wineskin is our new and fresh awareness. Let us shed yesterday's beliefs. This is an important concept and is repeated three times throughout the Bible.

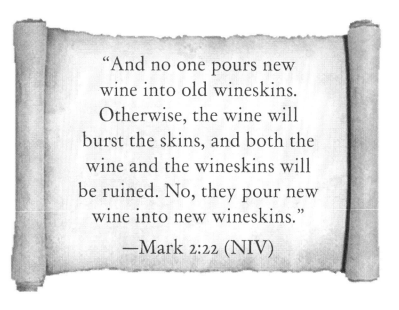

"And no one pours new wine into old wineskins. Otherwise, the wine will burst the skins, and both the wine and the wineskins will be ruined. No, they pour new wine into new wineskins."

—Mark 2:22 (NIV)

"And no one pours new
wine into old wineskins.
Otherwise, the new wine will
burst the skins; the wine will
run out and the wineskins
will be ruined."

—Luke 5:37 (NIV)

Chapter 13

THE POWER OF COMBINATION

> "**Ask**, and it will be given to you;
> **seek** and you will find; **knock** and
> the door will be opened to you.
> For everyone who asks receives;
> the one who seeks finds; and to
> the one who knocks, the door
> will be opened."
>
> —Matthew 7:7-8 (NIV)

Let us combine **thinking** the thought, **speaking** the word, and **writing** it down. When combined, we can knock **three times** on the door of God's Universe showing how serious we are, and success is guaranteed.

The Power Of Combination

As an example of showing what is possible when applying the combination of knocking three times on the door of God's Universe, here is a beautiful story from my teenage niece, who created her college life exactly as she desired it and more:

"As I required help paying for college, the question was what was I able to do about it. Going away to college and earning a four-year degree was important to me, so I did the first two things I thought of: pray and focus.

"I kept my grades up and visited my college advisor several times a week collecting information about colleges and other organizations and the scholarships they offered. I required a full-ride scholarship to make my dream of attending university a reality.

"Through research and information, I found out that the number of full-ride scholarships was becoming more rare. It was a tall order to have college completely paid for through scholarships and grants. The summer before my senior year, I sat down with my family and we prayed and declared that I receive a full-ride scholarship and more to the college that was right for me. Senior year began and I kept faith that God had a plan and applied for many colleges and scholarships.

"The advisor told me about two scholarships in particular. One was from a private organization offering $8,000 a year. The other was an invitation-only scholarship for housing or tuition at California State University Long Beach. Thus, I decided to apply there. I was chosen as the single nominee from my school to be considered for a private scholarship. I received both scholarships. The combination of the two scholarships and other grants has been more than enough to pay for all four years with extra money left for textbooks and school supplies.

"God's plan is certainly always perfect. This experience confirmed that God has a plan and His Universe will order things for our benefit and His glory. Numerous things lined up that were even beyond my asking. Many people have congratulated me for earning these scholarships, but I know that the credit goes to God and the miracles that He performs in our lives daily."

God's powerful Universe is full of such an abundance of resources that it is beyond our mind's comprehension. Let us keep **asking**.

Chapter 14

THE POWER OF THE MORPHIC FIELD

The Quantum World is all the particles around us, whereas the Morphic Field consists of the developed pathways energy travels along. It is the energy field created and used by our vibrations. The immediate energy grid surrounding us is called our Morphic Field. The Morphic Field is everywhere. It is influenced by our words and thoughts.

Let us imagine our Morphic Field as a vast field of tall grass. The energy vibrating in the grass is love. When we travel the same path back and forth, soon the grass is marked with our footprints. A clear path evolves from continuous travel. This clear path now is an imprinted route, which is easier and faster to traverse through than the rest of the grass field. In our brain, these routes are called neural pathways. Our repetitive thoughts and words cut these paths in our Morphic Field. They shape our lives. Here is another way to visualize the Morphic Field: we each have our own individual grid, our own unique spider web that we have woven with our repetitive habits, beliefs, and thoughts.

Let us consciously make sure that our paths are straight, accurate, blessed, and lead us to where we really desire to be. It is most efficient to form straight, direct, and conscious routes.

When we commit to walking only along our new consciously selected paths, we will head directly toward our goals and our God.

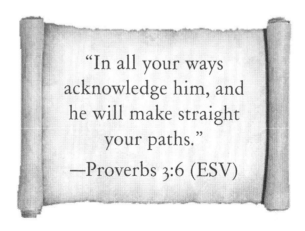

"In all your ways acknowledge him, and he will make straight your paths."
—Proverbs 3:6 (ESV)

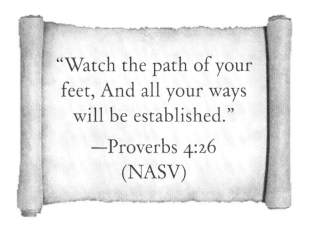

"Watch the path of your feet, And all your ways will be established."

—Proverbs 4:26 (NASV)

With positive thoughts and words as well as clearly focused and stated desires, **light and easy** pathways are formed. We consciously imprint new paths with trained effort until the new paths are familiar and more comfortable to travel than the old ones. We actively retrain our subconscious. We are positively reshaping our thinking.

The grass on the old paths will start to regrow until they are filled in. Now, our subconscious can use the new paths. Even when we are sleeping, it easily finds its way. Life is **light and easy** when we travel our rejoicing paths that lead to happiness and truth.

This is when life feels good and flows abundantly and our world is friendly.

Albert Einstein reminded us that doing the same thing over and over brings the same results. We have the choice to imprint our Morphic Field with our desired good. Let's do it!

Part Two

Seek!

Chapter 15

THE NINE STEPS TO RECEIVE

All my life I understood and felt easily connected to the Quantum World. It excited me, I played with it, and I called it in as my friend. I believed in it. I prayed to God who governs it. I depended on it and I leaned on it. I flowed with it. Everything appeared **light and easy** and exactly as I desired it all the time.

I always knew that there is a surrounding force in the world and it matches my own frequencies. We vibrate harmoniously. I have witnessed many miracles since I started to actively and consciously live fully aware in this friendly world of Quantum Physics, Light, and Vibrational Frequencies. I know it is my gift to make it **light and easy** for people to understand, connect with, and make use of this force, the Quantum World.

My life's work is to help people vibrate at a higher frequency, allowing their unique, personal vibrations to return to their intrinsic state and harmonically resonate with health. Each vibration becomes a more powerful life force.

I use harmonic waves to encourage balance between our personal vibrations and the universal frequencies. Changing our minds and beliefs, along with optimizing our words, will correct the vibrations we emit to the Universe. The Universe has a perfect language, and when we speak this language we have beautiful communication power.

My wish is to share my insights about the Quantum World with all humanity. I wish for everyone to understand the Power of the Universe. In this section, I present my simple-to-follow Nine Step recipe, allowing everyone to easily create their desired outcomes.

Our mission is to rediscover who we are and to regain control of our own experiences. Each of us can investigate our inner self and choose to bring glory to our life. When our consciousness is pure then God's perfect consciousness can and will enter—and light our lives. As I said earlier, God reminds us to be a new wineskin repeatedly in the Holy Bible.

Listed below are the Nine Steps to follow in order to consciously create:

1. **Connect**: Plug into God's Almighty **Gift**, the Power of the Universe, and discover your life's purpose.

2. **Declare**: Be clear about what you are truly seeking and ask for it.

   Have **Faith,** focus, and be courageous.

3. **Dominate**: Receive your inheritance and put on your crown.

   Believe.

4. **Be calm**: **Align** your head with your heart.

   Have **Peace**.

5. **Take action**: Focus on your breath and let the "how" be up to God.

   Let Him wow us with the "how." He does it.

6. **Lead with love**: Let us **love ourselves** first.

   Have **Grace**.

7. **Bless everyone** and **everything** with **love and gratitude.**

   Have **Mercy**.

8. **Expect the miracle in every moment**. Know the **Truth**.

   Be conscious of what you create and allow yourself to receive your desires.

9. **Have fun and celebrate**: Enjoy your creation and rejoice.

   Trust God.

Over the past 40 years, I have had plenty of occasions to play around and have fun with my creating. I once challenged myself to recreate an exact experience I had before. It was December, and a girlfriend had invited me to attend her office Christmas party. The party was held on a casino ship where we were invited to eat dinner and gamble.

Her company gave each employee and guest $50 to use to gamble with. My friend and I have little interest in gambling, and over dinner we discussed if gambling or keeping the money was more appealing to us. A memory came to me from a time years ago when I was in Las Vegas and at the last minute before leaving the casino, I put three dollar-coins into the slot machine and won the jackpot.

I had a fun thought to re-create this experience. I waited until they gave the final call for gambling, because the ship was docking shortly. I put my quarter in a slot machine and won the jackpot just as I had 25 years earlier in Las Vegas. In both of the experiences, I just pulled the lever once and won the jackpot. I modeled my behavior from my first success. I:

- ♥ matched the thought processes
- ♥ duplicated the philosophy I used just prior to winning the jackpot years ago
- ♥ stood the way I stood
- ♥ breathed the same way
- ♥ centered myself
- ♥ spoke the same words
- ♥ felt the same feeling
- ♥ chose to have absolute faith in my desired outcome

Chapter 16

STEP 1: CONNECT

If we have a wonderful electrical device, let us plug it in and connect it to an active power source. Only then is it useful.

We plug in the cord and connect. What if we are wonderful devices ourselves and we can connect to and harness all power? In order to make the most of our device—our earthly life—let us connect to the gift. Connect to His righteousness.

The strongest power source in this world is the Power of the Universe. God is the power. He is the Power of the Universe. He is the gift. He designed this Universe as a perfect delivery system already stocked with total abundance of love, happiness, health, and wealth. Our first choice and opportunity is to plug in and connect to Him!

"Seek ye **first** the Kingdom of Heaven (God) and his righteousness; and all these things shall be added unto you."
—Matthew 6:33 (KJV)

God promises us that, after we are plugged in, we receive two gifts. First, we will receive **His righteousness**. This means we receive His truth and the truth shall set us free. His truth is perfection; perfection of health, wealth, relationships, and wisdom. It sets us free to live peacefully, lovingly, kindly, and joyfully as well as boldly and courageously. The second gift we receive is "all **these things** shall be added" to us. What are THESE things? What THINGS?

In the Holy Bible, **God has left space in creation for each of us to write our own story**, our own list of "things." Are we clear on our goals and desires for our life?

 Picture the grand doors to your perfect life swinging open: what do they reveal? What are your life's dreams and desires?

This book will help to encourage you to create and define a direction and plan for your life.

Along the path of studying, working, marriage, raising children, and tending to loved ones, we might forget what lies behind our doors. With constant meditation and focus, we are able to visualize our own heart's desires more clearly. We all know that what we focus on we will receive more of. Thus, focus well.

Step 1: Connect

To begin, we can answer several questions for ourselves:

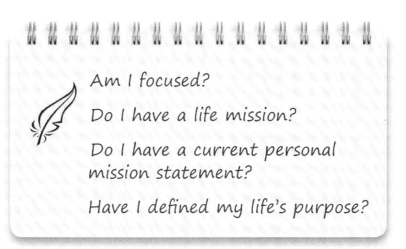

Am I focused?

Do I have a life mission?

Do I have a current personal mission statement?

Have I defined my life's purpose?

How do we even find our life's purpose? Everyone has a definite purpose in their life. It is important to take the time to acknowledge and then embrace our personal purpose. Let us explore and articulate our definite life's purpose. To find our life's purpose, we start by being aware of what we enjoy. This will enable us to define ourselves.

Start with an awareness of what you enjoy. The following questions will help guide you to re-discover yourself.

Are you an indoor person or an outdoor person?

Do you enjoy living in the city or outside the city?

Do you prefer the ocean or the mountains?

Do you prefer a beach house or a cabin in the woods?

Do you like warm weather or cold weather?

Sunshine, rain, or snow?

The tropics or the desert?

What is your favorite season?

If you can live anywhere in the world, where will it be?

Step 1: Connect

If you have a second home, where will it be?

Do you prefer animals or people?

Do you prefer to be with other people or to be alone?

Do you enjoy working with youth or the elderly?

What talents do you have?

What are your hobbies?

What sports do you enjoy?

Do you prefer music or dancing?

Do you like listening to music or playing music yourself?

Do you enjoy taking pictures or making home movies?

Do you prefer reading or watching movies?

Do you enjoy learning or teaching?

Are you are seminar enthusiast?

Do you enjoy making or eating food?

Cooking or baking?

Do you enjoy spa treatments?

Are you the giver or receiver of the spa treatments? Or both?

Do you prefer to give time or money to a charitable cause?

What types of charities are you attracted to?

What are you good at?

What truly makes you happy?

What do you do for fun?

What do you do for hours and it seems like only minutes?

What causes you to jump out of bed energetically and enthusiastically in the morning?

Step 1: Connect

This is your passion!

Start collecting data on yourself. Start collecting data on your personal happiness. Write your own "Fun List"! This list contains things that make your heart sing.

Next, create a second list of "Who I am" and then a third list of "My ideal self." This list contains every attribute of who you desire to be. Continually add to your lists.

Now, circle the top five most important words on your lists.

Formulate your mission statement using these five words.

The following easy format will help you:

"My divine mission is to _____
_____

for/with myself and others."

For example:

"My divine mission is to give and receive joy and experience health for myself and others through rediscovering the truth."

"My divine mission is to share happiness with the Universe."

If we are ordering a pizza, we tell the person taking our order our exact desires. Do we like cheese crust? Do we prefer extra toppings? Are we a meat lover? Do we prefer only vegetables?

Often, in our life's pizza parlor, we just walk in,

sit down, and talk to our friends without placing an order, because they have already ordered their pizza. When that pizza is served, we end up eating someone else's pizza, even if we honestly prefer a different pizza for ourselves. Let us always order our own pizza with all the delicious toppings we wish for.

When a friend of mine from the Miracle Group was pondering what to do next with her life, she prayed for guidance and asked God, "What shall I do? Show me in a way that I will understand."

Shortly after, she was with a friend who was experiencing strong sensations in his back and she offered to massage him. After the massage was done, the friend asked her if she gave massages professionally. This sparked a new idea. He told her, "You give an amazing massage. Please become a massage therapist."

My friend liked the idea and went online to search for schools and tuition fees. She emailed many schools. One school called her the same day and invited her for an interview. The representatives of the school explained the program and my friend told them her vision. She was accepted immediately.

She inquired about the cost, which was $22,000. She thanked the gentlemen very much and said that she required time to consider this type of investment.

He said the school had a financial aid department and suggested she stop there to inquire if it was possible for her to obtain a loan.

She applied, was accepted, received a loan that very day, and the classes started the following week. She was also enrolled in the best class they offered. The more time she spent at the school, the more she liked it. She often thought to herself, "This is my thing! It feels so good." Now, she is a licensed massage therapist.

Let us open our minds and hearts in prayer and allow God to speak to us and ask Him to assist us with our life's purpose.

When my kids were very young, we moved into a new house. They were jumping on our new king-size bed. They were yelling with joy, "We are so glad we are millionaires. It's so much fun to be a millionaire!"

The patio door was wide open. As I entered the room, I heard their loud energetic voices declaring their desires. I thought for a very brief moment, "What are the neighbors going to think?" One second later, I corrected my thought, "Let them chant and create whatever they desire in their ingenious lives."

I wondered, at their ages of one, three, and four if they even knew what a millionaire is. Fifteen years later, it is reality; they are millionaires. God wishes us to joyously declare whatever is our heart's desire. Sing it; dance it; jump on a bed!

Let us check that we remain connected to God throughout the day through prayer. Be encouraged to further develop a personal relationship with God. Once we invite Him into our heart, ask Him to stay here all day long. Let us keep our channel of communication open to Him. Once we are connected and the channel is open, we are plugged in and will continue to prosper. Now we are set up to **ask and receive**.

> " 'For I know the plans I have for you,' declares the LORD, 'plans to **prosper** you and not to harm you, plans to **give you hope and a future.** '"
>
> —Jeremiah 29:11 (NIV)

Chapter 17

STEP 2: DECLARE

A navigation system using the Global Position System (GPS) is very beneficial; it guides us and keeps us on track. The device is a receiver for unique signals emitted from 24 satellites orbiting the Earth.

When we enter an exact address in the navigation system, the GPS signal first helps us to determine our location and then finds ways to our destination. It provides the "how" to arrive there. To reach a definite location, we enter in every detail of the address, starting with the country, then adding the state, city, and street, including the street number. If anything is left out, we might end up in a different place.

The same holds true for our creations. We shall ask in detailed declaration. The more detail we add in, the faster and more accurately we reach our targeted outcome. God is our GPS for life! We supply the address (detailed goals). He supplies the guidance and the path to achieve our destination (goals).

Once we are plugged in and have declared an exact address in our navigation system, whichever way we turn in life, we will end up at our desired destination. If we miss a turn anywhere along the way, it will lead us back to the right path toward our destination. We can make as many stops as we wish along our life's journey; eventually we will arrive at our destination.

Let us **ask** by declaring our desires. Remember, every word counts. Everything happens when we ask. The Universe gently flows and waits until we organize our thoughts and ask. Then it goes into action and shakes out whatever we order.

It pulls from all its resources of all existence: past, present, and future. It combines and processes our order. Total focused intention, coupled with strong positive will, leads to fast delivery. The clearer and more detailed we are with our orders, the more we will recognize them and truly know that they are ours when they appear.

In our Miracle Group, one member had us second the motion for her to regain contact with an old friend who moved away. She desired her friend's forwarding information.

A week later, she received a Christmas card from this friend that had her new mailing information on the envelope. Now they are back in contact. When we ask with a clear intention, we receive a fast answer.

The question then becomes: What do we honestly desire? We are the authors of our life. Anything worth doing is worth writing about first. Thomas Edison filled over 1,000 notebooks with his thoughts, words, and diagrams. We still have notebooks from Leonardo da Vinci. All his genius is recorded on paper, pages upon pages.

It is often said that success leaves clues. People who we recognize as successful all wrote their ideas down. We certainly are thankful the Bible was written down. Of all the glory God left us, the most important thing He left us in physical form is the Bible and when we open it up, it is full of words. Knock three times: Think the thought, speak the word, and write it down. It is proven that the most successful people write everything down, thus calling it into existence.

Step 2: Declare

A study conducted by psychology professor Dr. Gail Matthews at Dominican University in San Rafael, California and presented in 2015, reported that those participants who wrote down their goals accomplished significantly more than those who refrained from putting them in writing.

Let us take paper with us everywhere we go or carry a journal. If all we have is ourselves, we can use our finger as a pen and the air as the paper. Let us always write it down.

A friend of mine shared his story of manifesting his dream. When he first moved to England, he took a two-week vacation and toured five countries. After arriving in Lucerne, Switzerland, he saw the picturesque mountains overlooking a peaceful lake and **he declared**, "One day I will live here."

Upon returning to England, he met his lovely wife who was born and raised in Lucerne, Switzerland. Now, after living 50 years in England, they are retired and living happily in Lucerne.

My condo was on the market for four months. I knew exactly why it was still for sale. I was mentally attached to the condo. In a thoughtful moment, I made up my mind to finally release it. I asked myself what my conditions to release it were.

First, the buyers will love it as much as I do. Second, they will pay the asking price in cash. And third, they will move in immediately, making certain that I will honor the sale.

I declared my three desired parameters in writing, sank down on my knees, and prayed over them as I went to bed at 11:30 p.m. The next morning at 8:30 my real estate agent called saying my condo had an offer on it for my asking price, the buyers were willing to pay cash, and they desired to move in in three days. They still live there today and love the condo as much as I did.

A few years after my condo sold, neighbors from my new neighborhood were visiting me and they told me their house had been on the market for months and they really desired it to sell. I shared the story of my condo selling overnight.

They immediately went home, wrote down that the house is already sold. They visualized it sold and imagined how excited they were in their new house. Their house sold the same week, and they joyfully came over to tell me that the Nine Step Method really works!

Step 2: Declare

Act in total faith and be courageous. God served my sister a lesson of faith as she was walking Daytona Beach:

A woman walking toward her called out to watch for whales far out on the horizon. That sounded wonderful to her. She dearly loves seeing wildlife on beach walks. She diligently scanned the horizon. Where were the whales?

She proceeded on her walk, enjoying the fresh air, sand, and surf. She playfully declared to God and His powerful Universe her deep desire to see a whale. "However," she said to him, "with my eyesight, God please help me by bringing the whale a whole lot closer than the horizon for me to see!"

She continued to walk and slowly became aware of what she thought was a dolphin paralleling her walk, traveling only slightly faster than she, giving her ample opportunity to observe and appreciate it. It appeared to be a very large black dolphin, unique to any she had seen before. It cruised straight through the waves with its head, fin, and back continually exposed, significantly different than the typical way dolphins swim.

She reveled in this sighting, enjoying and studying it as a new experience. She walked with the mammal; the sand, beach, and other walkers around her were completely forgotten. My sister left the beach that morning praising the Lord for all the fantastic wildlife He had shared with her, including the dolphin that swim close along the shore.

God most likely was shaking His head, chuckling to Himself, and asking, "How much more obvious can I make this for her?" Two days later, upon her return to town, she read, in one of the local newspapers, an article mentioning the rare presence on the coast of a large number of small black whales. The article included a photo.

There in the photo was an entire pod of her very black, very large "dolphins." God's Universe is indeed precise and powerful!

Can we have total faith to accept the desired "whale" or do we settle for the "dolphin"? Can we go for the gold all the time? There is so much faith. Faith is everywhere. It is free.

We can lean on God and others if our faith requires recharging. Rightminded positive people re-ignite our faith.

My sister's whale story inspired a friend from my Miracle Group to be more courageous. After hearing this story, my girlfriend declared to all her friends in her Miracle Group, "I will sell my house for more than the asking price."

Step 2: Declare

She also declared it to her agent, who told her that she had priced her house as the most expensive house in the neighborhood and pleaded with her to reconsider the price. The house was decorated in a European style with much love for detail.

My friend really desired to sell her house and make extra money for a Qi Gong retreat she wished to attend. The final payment was due within a week.

She replied, "This is my house and I will ask whatever price I desire. In fact, I will sell it for more than the asking price."

Two interested parties came to see the house and fell in love with it. One gave an offer right away. As the second party was ready to hand in their offer, my friend told them, "I already have an offer. Make me your best offer."

The offer the second party made was $8,000 more than the original asking price. This extra money was more than enough to pay for the Qi Gong retreat. Her story may be a boost for everyone reading it to have greater faith and courage.

"Therefore, since we have been justified through **faith**, we have peace with God through our Lord Jesus Christ, through whom we have gained access by **faith** into this grace in which we now stand. And we boast in the hope of the **glory of God**."

—Romans 5:2 (NIV)

Chapter 18

STEP 3: DOMINATE

We are created and born to win—more than just the first and second quarter of the game—the whole game. We are winners. We deserve the feeling of triumph, success, and accomplishment. Our vibrational field is set up to triumph over everything.

We all start out at our best; 100 percent perfect! The only obstacles detouring us from successfully achieving our accomplishments are our own thoughts.

In the first page of the Bible, God gave us dominion over the Earth.

"Then God said, 'Let Us make men in Our image, according to Our likeness; let them have **dominion** over the fish of the sea, over the birds of the air, and over the cattle, over all the earth and over every creeping thing that creeps on the earth.'"

—Genesis 1:26 (NKJV)

Again, in Genesis 1:28:

"And God blessed them, and God said unto them, Be fruitful, and multiply, and replenish the earth, and subdue it: and have **dominion** over the fish of the sea, and over the fowl of the air, and over every living thing that moveth upon the earth."

—Genesis 1:28 (KJV)

Twice, He repeated His desire for us to rule over this Earth, to show us how important this was to Him. God gave us this life to **reign**. We are the **children of God**. I serve a very big God. How about you? My God delivers 100 percent of the time. With Him success is guaranteed. God shows up in a huge way. He is a miracle maker. The only way He works is supernaturally.

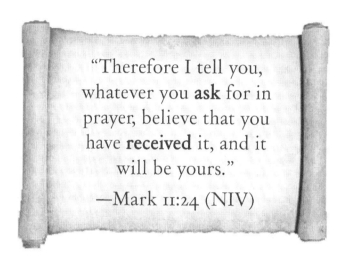

"Therefore I tell you, whatever you **ask** for in prayer, believe that you have **received** it, and it will be yours."

—Mark 11:24 (NIV)

It is our birthright to **dominate**. We deserve whatever good we consciously ask for.

Let us put our crown back on and the world will bow. Let us walk in our inheritance. Let us honor Him with it. If we buy our kids new shoes, we receive great joy when we see them wearing their new shoes.

Let us envision ourselves having **Breakfast with God.** We sit down with our Heavenly Father at the table. We are His children.

"The Spirit himself testifies with our spirit that we are God's children."

—Romans 8:16 (NIV)

God is King, so we are all princes and princesses.

"Do not be afraid, little flock, for your Father has been pleased to give you the kingdom."

—Luke 12:32 (NIV)

Step 3: Dominate

And He said:

"Truly I tell you, unless you change and become like little children, you will never enter the kingdom of heaven."

—Matthew 18:3 (NIV)

Let us put our royal cape on, wear our crowns and keep our signet ring on our finger. As we sit down with our Abba Father, he will ask us, "What are your plans for today?" We share with Him the things we intend to enjoy doing today.

He will also ask us what grand plans we have for our future. Let us tell him our desires, our biggest plans, and ask him for help. When breakfast is finished He blesses us, "Go in love and have fun!" As we go through our day, let us do so with authority, have fun, and keep our crown on. We are free to enjoy this day. Leave the bigger plans and the "how" it will happen for God to create.

If we lose our glory for a moment, we just stand back up and put our crown back on. He reminds us to keep our royal crown on at all times. Then He can see us and be with us throughout the day.

Most mornings I stand as I am leaving the breakfast table and say, "I leave it up to you God to WOW ME!"

Every single day is a new creation; every day we are new.

In the morning, LORD,
you hear my voice;
**in the morning I lay my
requests before you** and
wait expectantly.
—Psalm 5:3 (NIV)

Every morning, let us lay out a new white tablecloth to have Breakfast with God. Yesterday's tablecloth is rolled up and thrown out.

Please ask yourself:

What shall I do differently today to allow more peace in my life?

What am I willing to empty from my pockets before starting new?

What if this is the only day I have? What will it look like?

"Therefore, if anyone is in Christ, he is a new creation. The old has passed away; behold, the new has come."

—II Corinthians 5:17 (NIV)

An investor was instituting legal proceedings against my friend's husband and his two partners on a stagnant investment. This lawsuit was for $600,000. My friend had adamantly written down that they were going to win a financial settlement she can handle. That was all there was to it. It was moving her way and she said, "I shall settle today, because **I can accomplish everything I desire**." Period.

This lawsuit was to be settled even before choosing the jury. When they arrived at court that day, the other party offered to settle for $300,000. They all convened in the hallway. The two partners said, "No way." They went back into court.

The attorneys were trying to keep it from going to trial. Their next offer was $200,000. The two partners said, "No, we will go to trial." They were ready to choose the jury at that point when the defendants made one last settlement attempt for $100,000. Split three ways, $33,333.33 was her only obligation. Her side accepted. And the case was settled out of court. It ended quite favorably as she had asked.

A friend's husband had invested in a piece of property. When the economy collapsed in 2008 and property values plummeted, the property was now worth about 10 cent on the dollar. The bank was owed $100,000 on a property now worth $10,000. There was little means for paying this amount owed to the bank. My friend's husband was forced to close his office and was no longer able to communicate with investors or bankers.

Consequently, he depended on his wife to negotiate on his behalf. The bank desired this project off of their books. They were seeking some kind of fair settlement. The banker called my friend one day and said, "Just offer something ridiculous." She said, "What does that mean?" And he repeated, "Just make an offer, a ridiculous offer."

She questioned what a ridiculous offer on a $100,000 debt was. She asked a couple of business friends who suggested $10,000 to $15,000 as a fair offer. Her creation power kicked in at that point and she declared that her ridiculous offer was $2,500. The banker said, "I'll check with my people and call you back."

The next day he called to say, "They accepted your offer of $2,500." A miracle for sure.

My daughter took German in college for one semester. One day, after taking an exam, she returned home and realized she had forgotten to turn it in. She was almost in tears because she had studied so diligently for the test. She asked me, "Mom, what can I do?" I asked her, "What are you seeking?" She replied, "I wish for this test to be handed in to the teacher." I encouraged her to state her ultimate desire:

"Do you think God requires a piece of paper to give you an "A"? Is 100 percent in the grade book what you are really looking for?"

She answered, "Yes, Mom." I proposed, "Let us ask God and His Universe in writing for 100 percent in the grade book." She wrote it down.

Two weeks later, when the teacher handed back the test, she said to my daughter, "I am missing your test. I know you were here and since you are the best student in the class I put 100 percent in the grade book." The words the teacher spoke back to my daughter are the exact words she wrote down. **As you believe and ask, so shall it be.**

Chapter 19

STEP 4: BE CALM—ALIGN YOUR HEAD WITH YOUR HEART

This is the most important step.

In order to attract or manifest, the calmer we are and the more peace we welcome into our life, the easier things flow toward us. The more peaceful and calm we are, the more we increase our ability to receive.

Let us be in a relaxed state to recognize and receive our blessings. Let us align our emotions with our desired feelings, allowing both to head in the same direction. The road of creation flows in one direction only. The Universe is divinely inspired to flow with a hypnotic rhythm in one direction.

In nature everything flows in one direction at a

time: For example, the planets rotate and revolve in only one direction, vines grow consistently in the same direction around a tree, and rivers flow from the mountains to the sea or a lake.

Our emotions may tend to be affected by other people with our desire to please them while our gut feelings are attached to God's Almighty Power. Honoring our first gut feeling is an area where most of us can use practice.

We know what is right for us. Let us stay true to our righteous gut feelings. Let us find our true North and head in that direction. Let us choose to develop a clear awareness by paying renewed attention to our gut.

As mentioned before, the fastest way to receive anything is to knock three times: **Think the thought, speak the word, and write it down in positive words.**

After we have ordered our desires from the Ether in this manner, temporarily forget about them and relax. Becoming calm allows our mind and body to enter a peaceful state of neutrality.

There is wonder in this step. Sit back and relax; your order has been sent out and confirmed. The delivery is on its way. It is as easy as dining out at a restaurant: we choose our food from the menu, place our order, relax, and just expect the order to show up.

Step 4: Be Calm

Does wondering if our food will be delivered have an influence on the speed of delivery? Most often we are so busy talking to our friends that our food just shows up. When it comes, we may even be surprised at what we ordered.

I am often asked if it is necessary to **ask** repetitively to reaffirm the same request. Remember times when we are in the car and the kids keep asking every three minutes, "Are we there yet?" Their repetitive asking has zero influence on how fast we arrive. God has perfect hearing. He hears us the first time. We are His children.

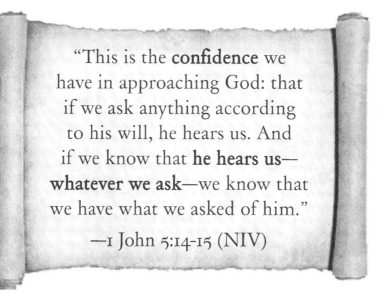

"This is the **confidence** we have in approaching God: that if we ask anything according to his will, he hears us. And if we know that **he hears us—whatever we ask**—we know that we have what we asked of him."

—1 John 5:14-15 (NIV)

Ask And You Shall Receive

The question is: Do we have enough confidence in ourselves to listen to ourselves?

Whenever my youngest daughter loses something, **she keeps very calm**. For example, she has a small souvenir rock the size of a thumb from Belize that she values a lot. She has lost it many times, because she carries it around in her pocket and sets it down in places.

Over the years, it has been lost in the car or in hotel rooms. Whenever this happens, she tells herself, "It's okay, I'll find it." Many times lost and found, she still has the rock to this day.

A woman in my town was contacted by the county and asked to remove certain bushes because they were outlawed recently. She inquired as to who was to pay for their removal. She was told that she herself was responsible to pay the expenses. She hung up the phone. **She calmed herself**, focused her thoughts, called the county back, and declared to them that they may happily remove the bushes for free and enhance her yard. She was told by the county to take care of it herself.

The next morning, county workers rang her doorbell and she saw that the bushes had been removed and new plants had been put in their place for free. Her calm confidence attracted her desire immediately.

Step 4: Be Calm

Let us transmit our ideas with clarity to the Universe. Building a safety net or having a "plan B" may confuse the process. Continuously have confidence in our declared goals; otherwise we may create and call in confusion.

Our "just in case" plans B, C, D, and so on are only there to make us feel better; God always creates it right the first time. The calmer we are, the more clearly our frequencies transmit.

Let us focus on our breath, relax our breathing, smile and keep calm, let it go, and let life flow. Be in peace. All is well.

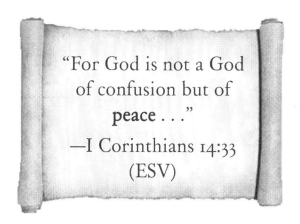

"For God is not a God
of confusion but of
peace . . ."
—I Corinthians 14:33
(ESV)

Chapter 20

STEP 5: TAKE ACTION—FOCUS ON YOUR BREATH

It is our joy in this creation to call in what we do desire. As with a satellite signal, if our GPS is out of range, sometimes all that is necessary is to move our car just a bit to receive the signal. If we feel that we are disconnected in any way from the Power and we feel that we desire help to receive the signal, we can simply exhale and gently relax.

Any action we take is a perfect action. I simply exhale. This calming motion helps regain neutrality. Let us be aware of our breath in the moment. Let us take three deep breaths and focus only on our inhalation and our exhalation.

Step 5: Take Action

Let us do it right now! Relax and soften your shoulders. Gently touch your tongue to the roof of your mouth. Breathe in and out through the nose. Take a full breath deep in your diaphragm. Push your belly out as you inhale. Push your bottom down into your chair. Imagine the oxygen reaching every cell in your body. Softly hold your breath a short moment. Flatten your belly as you gently exhale. Relax your shoulders even more.

Repeat this breathing pattern three times. Inhale deeply. Exhale fully. Inhale deeply. Exhale fully. Inhale deeply. Exhale fully. Throughout the day repeat this pattern as often as you wish.

When we breathe deeply into our diaphragm, the lymph system is able to move the toxins out of our system. In this sense, deep breathing will move both our physical waste and our mental waste, helping us to become more calm. Lack of peace makes our body acidic, whereas being aligned and calm enhances the alkaline state of the body.

Most of our bodily functions, such as our digestion, are beautifully maintained when the body is alkaline. Being in constant fight-or-flight mode may keep us acidic. The frontal lobe is the area of the brain responsible for decision-making. It functions best when we are calm.

God is in our breath. God gave us the breath of life as our first gift.

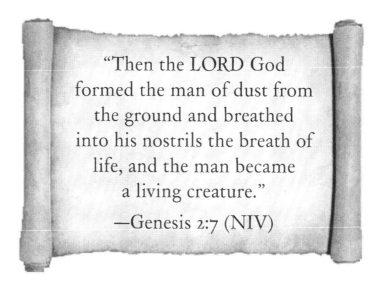

"Then the LORD God formed the man of dust from the ground and breathed into his nostrils the breath of life, and the man became a living creature."
—Genesis 2:7 (NIV)

This breath of life is Source Light Energy.

God is with us now in each breath and He is with

us only now, because there only is now. Relax, let go, and let God embrace us. Remember, God created us as human beings. Somehow we reimagined ourselves as human doings.

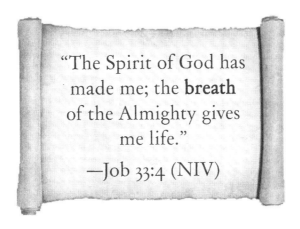

"The Spirit of God has made me; the **breath** of the Almighty gives me life."

—Job 33:4 (NIV)

Once we have completed the first four steps, our order is placed. **How** it will be delivered **is up to God**. How it comes to us is least important; most important is that we allow ourselves to receive our goals.

This is beautifully demonstrated in the "Parable of the Growing Seed" in Mark 4:

> "He also said, 'This is what the kingdom of God is like. A man scatters seed on the ground. Night and day, whether he sleeps or gets up, the seed sprouts and grows, though he **does not know how.** All by itself the soil produces grain—first the stalk, then the head, then the full kernel in the head. As soon as the grain is ripe, he puts the sickle to it, because the harvest has come.'"
>
> —Mark 4:26-34 (NIV)

When the Christmas season was just about a month away and I was thinking about all the goodies being served, I decided to give my body a chance to rest and relax. I started a detox in which I only drank fresh pressed green juices. I juice once in a while, because I really like the energy and the taste of green juices; however, cleaning the juicer is less than appealing to me; and sometimes the blade sticks. This drew my attention to the new juicers now available.

One company I researched offered a chance to win a free juicer. I entered the competition, then I wrote down in declaration, "I have a new fancy juicer for free that is really easy to clean."

The next morning, I visited one of my friends and we talked about her new focus on minimalism and how she currently wished to keep only what she really uses regularly in her house. She told me that she had decided to give away her fancy juicer. She had only used it three times, because she prefers her blender. That day I won my free, easy-to-clean juicer from my girlfriend!

After we place our order, let us relax and surrender, knowing that the Universe has the "how" in the works. Let us release all our thoughts regarding our order and **trust that it will be delivered**.

One night, many years ago, I was dressed to go out with my friends as a snow storm dropped six inches of fresh snow on our Wisconsin home. As I was about to leave the house, my mother asked me, "Are you going somewhere? The driveway is snowed in and our street is full of snow!" I calmly declared my desire to go dancing and prayed for a quick resolution.

Then I put on my boots, grabbed a shovel, stood in the driveway, saw the city snowplow coming by, whistled loudly, and waved my arm to direct them up our driveway. With one sweep, our driveway was plowed. Then the snowplow went back on the road to plow our street.

I immediately walked back inside and switched from my boots to my dancing shoes. My mother asked me, "Are you done shoveling the driveway already?" I replied, "It's all done." She went to the door and to her amazement found our driveway plowed and the street clear. All she said to me was, "You've done it again." With a smile on my face, I went dancing.

After we place numerous orders, we are in practice and our trust in the Universe will continually develop. Just breathe; all that is required is to be calm and to breathe.

"**Give thanks** to the LORD, for he is **good**; his love endures forever."

—Psalm 118:1 (NIV)

This Psalm marks the middle of the Bible and reminds us to sing praises unto Him. Let us "Hymn Him" daily and watch our life grow miraculously!

Every loving aligned action taken to bless and be blessed through word or deed is the perfect action. Let love power us.

Chapter 21

STEP 6: LEAD WITH LOVE—LET US LOVE OURSELVES FIRST

The first commandment in the New Testament says:

> "Love the Lord your God
> with all your heart and
> with all your soul and with
> all your mind and with all
> your strength."
>
> —Mark 12:30 (NIV)

Step 6: Lead With Love

The second commandment in the New Testament says:

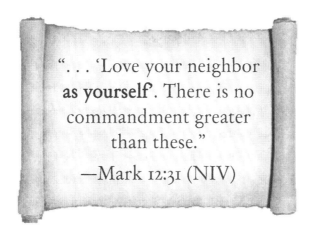

"... 'Love your neighbor **as yourself**'. There is no commandment greater than these."
—Mark 12:31 (NIV)

After fulfilling the first commandment, let us concentrate on the second one. **Love yourself first** in order to love others.

Prior to an airplane taking off, the flight attendant reminds us that in the event of an emergency to first put on our air mask before we assist others. Why do the airlines remind us to help ourselves first?

Another example to show this is through using our bank account. Money is first deposited in our account before writing good checks. Yet another way to put this: we can only jump in after a swimmer to rescue them if we are capable swimmers ourselves. First our cup shall be full, before it runneth over.

This demonstrates that the latter part of God's second commandment, "as you love yourself," is mandatory before we can fulfill the first part of the commandment. Are we loving ourselves so that our neighbors can be blessed?

When I shared this step with my sister, she humorously responded by saying, "Oh, my *poor* neighbor. I am so busy taking care of everyone else, I spend little time loving myself."

How about the rest of us? Are we taking enough time and are we making a continual effort to truly love ourselves? We can only love our neighbors as much as we love ourselves.

We are our own most critical judges. Instead, let us be our biggest fans. We have to cheer for ourselves. Go me! Go me! Remember, we are exactly where we are meant to be in every moment.

Stand in front of your mirror each day and tell yourself such things as:

"I love you. I am beautiful (handsome). I am awesome. I am a genius. I am happy. I am healthy. I live in a friendly world. I create great things. I am wealthy. I am fulfilled. I am perfect. God loves me."

Always smile at yourself. Be kind to yourself, accept what is and joyfully own your physical body!

Let us be our own cheerleader. Practice being happy and content alone with ourselves, because there is only me and my God in my hall of mirrors; what I create is reflected back to me. That is how we came into this world and how we will go out.

Let us start practicing being alone with God in joy. Let us be comfortable with ourselves. Let us feel good about ourselves. Let us be connected to our inner self. Let us be in tune. Let us appreciate ourselves. Let us know our value. Let us allow ourselves to be worthy of His Heavenly Kingdom. God made us worthy. We deserve everything we desire. Our desires desire us.

Everyone is perfect all the time. We are one humanity. God's almighty Holy Spirit within us loves us. The Holy Spirit in us loves all. Love is who we are; anything less is an illusion.

> *If you desire encouragement, tell yourself how great you are. Ask others to remind you of your greatness. You can also use our Receive Joy meditations, affirmations and inspirations.*

Since we have total control over our emotional choices, we first shall understand that love is our option. Believing and having faith in ourselves is a choice. Whatever stands in front of us in our lives, we always have choices, because we always have control over our actions and reactions.

Where we focus our intention is our choice and most important decision. Focus on the delicious, plump, juicy, full bunches of grapes in our lives and leave the dry shriveled raisins alone. Focus on the positive charge of every atom. The negative charge is mandatory for the balance of the Universe. It is our choice where our focus goes.

The **attitude** we choose while we focus makes a big difference. The emotion we put behind our focused intentions accelerates or slows down the receiving process.

One day, when I was in the middle of my Five Minute Couch Time (discussed in detail in Part Three), an interesting thought came to me: I love myself so much, I deserve loving neighbors. They love me. How can I create loving neighbors? Maybe my focus, when I moved in more than 15 years ago, was internal, but now I choose to broaden my blessings and start over.

Because I practiced to love myself so much over the years, I asked the Universe to allow whatever is necessary for my neighbors to love me as much as I love myself. The very next morning, a "for sale" sign went up in their yard. Those former neighbors desirably moved away. I love my new neighbors and they love me.

Ask And You Shall Receive

The more we love ourselves, the friendlier our world becomes. Let us love ourselves with grace.

Chapter 22

STEP 7: BLESS EVERYONE AND EVERYTHING WITH LOVE AND GRATITUDE

Dr. Emoto's work with water samples shows us that all water in and around us is imprintable. Thus, with our kind words and positive intentions our world has the opportunity to be transformed into a kind, loving, friendly place.

 To do this, bless everyone and everything with love and gratitude by saying:

"Thank you and bless you God, thank you and bless you family, thank you and bless you friends. Thank you and bless you my country. Thank you and bless you all humanity. I love you."

Bless all water to imprint it with good:

"Thank you, water, thank you, oceans, ponds, lakes, rivers, and streams. You are beautiful."

Bless nature:

Say "I love you" to the animals, the trees, the plants, the grounds, and all of nature surrounding us.

Bless everything as it serves us throughout the day:

"Thank you, beautiful water, for hydrating me. Thank you, bed, for my comfortable rest. Thank you, chair, for supporting me. Thank you, computer, for assisting me. I love and thank you, tree, for providing shade. I am grateful for the roof over my head. I love you, house, you serve me well," and so on. Bless all objects and thank them for their service in your life.

Go even further and name everything: Name your car, your plants, and your house as well as everything in it and everything you own. Naming everything creates love toward it. Let us imprint love everywhere.

A client of mine told me that the paperwork on her desk was stacking up more and more. She told herself, "I have to clean my desk" every time she saw it. The reason it was still awaiting her was that the task had little appeal and excitement.

After I shared this step with her, she went home and started to say, "I love you" to all her papers and her desk. She simply changed her thoughts and spoke kind words whenever she walked past her desk.

By the following weekend, she had spoken enough love and joy over it that she sat down and cleared her entire desk. The women called me afterward to tell me that she was amazed how easy the experience was. She is happy and delighted that she cleaned it all up and invited me over to see her neat desk.

Love and **gratitude** are vibrationally two of the strongest positive words on Earth. When frozen by Dr. Emoto and his team, each word forms the most beautiful water crystals and even more so when combined. Water showed Dr. Emoto that the powerful vibrations of sincere love and gratitude create a strong resonance that will purify or restructure water into balance and harmony. The pure vibrational resonance of the words love and gratitude have effects similar to the vibrations high frequency electrolysis devices have on purifying water.

Step 7: Bless Everyone And Everything

When we decide to focus on love and gratitude, it immediately changes our emotional state. When we decide to look at every event or person with love and gratitude, our feelings toward them can only be positive. Again, it is our choice to bless everything and everyone. Remember, all that is in our lives, be it in the past, present, or future, is of our co-creation.

Please take a moment to make a list of all that you are grateful for in this moment and add to it continually. Always remember to even be thankful for the obvious: Do you have eyes to see the beauty around you? Do you have a mouth to speak blessings? Do you have ears to listen to the joy that surrounds you? Do you have feet to walk on? Do you have a heart to love?

Let us have fun with another writing exercise. I call it **Praying Through Our Life.**

Fold a paper in half vertically. Open it up again. In the left margin, list everyone in your life. In the right margin next to their name, identify the greatest blessing they have brought to you. Write one or two good words that define the blessing of that person in your life.

For example, when I think of my mother, I think of "loving and caring." And when I think of my father, "giver" comes to my mind immediately.

After you are done with the list, pray these words over each person in true gratitude and make a habit of thanking them for their blessing in your life.

"Dear God, thank you for _____ (name) in my life, and thank you for their gift of _____ (words). Use all the energy around our relationship for the greater good and leave me with their gift of _____ (words)."

Whenever you desire encouragement and joy, pull out that list, fold it in half vertically and concentrate on the right column of all the blessings that fill your life.

To take this game a step further—and make it even more fun—take a pack of small note cards and write a single blessing one each one. Punch a hole in the corner and string them on a necklace. Wear the necklace and feel all the blessings in your life penetrate your heart.

The following is my friend's story, shared as a true reminder that the first step in any manifestation is to come from a place of gratitude:

"Shortly after our move to St. Petersburg, Florida, in 1999, my wonderful husband gifted me with a beautiful 3 carat marquise diamond ring. He saw it in the window of the jewelry store near our favorite grocery provider and invited me to go and take a look. Of course, I, like most women, said yes to such a gesture and went home with my new beautiful ring.

"We moved to New Mexico in 2009 and five years later, we were back visiting Florida to see friends. My husband again walked by the same jewelry store and saw a lovely diamond ring in the same window. I was the only one who knew my longing for a pear-shaped diamond ring, as I appreciated with great love the magnificent ring I had.

"He returned to our friend's home where we were staying and excitedly told me, 'Let us go back to "our" jewelry store and bring the checkbook.' The lovely 3 carat pear-shaped diamond ring fit perfectly on my hand. The jeweler had just put the ring in the window the previous day and was happy to take my marquise diamond ring in trade for a small payment.

"I gratefully and joyfully walked out of the store with the sparkling ring on my finger. It was such a loving gesture from my husband and it reminds me every day to be grateful for all the blessings I have in my life."

*Create simple ways to be a blessing to everyone around you. Partake in simple **acts of kindness** daily.*

Write a note of thank you or a kind note on the memo line on every check you write and every credit card receipt you sign.

Acknowledge the people you meet throughout the day. Smile and say hello to everyone you see, even those standing next to you in the elevator.

Wave at the parking attendants as you drive by the gatehouse. Choose to be friendly with people who are serving you. Allow somebody with fewer items to check out in front of you at the register. When driving, happily allow the car next to you to merge in front of your car. Smile and give a thank-you wave when somebody lets you merge in front of them.

On the way into the store, return an empty shopping cart and push the cart to the storefront when you are done. Pick up trash when you see it lying around. Open the door for the elderly— or anybody. Offer your seat on the bus. Gentlemen, please open the car doors for the ladies. Tell the person next to you how lovely they look today. Hug freely; hug a friend. Say thank you for every little thing someone does for you. Pray with someone on the spot. Send notes, cards, or kind, encouraging text messages throughout the day. A few positive, kind words go a long way.

Train yourself to be a good listener. God gave us two ears and one mouth. Let us use them accordingly. Let us share our love with acts of simple service, listening, and encouraging. People recognize the blessing. Then relax, sit back, and watch the love and gratitude flow back into your life.

Step 7: Bless Everyone And Everything

Years ago my sister experienced a significant simple act of kindness and she has been passing it on ever since. Her girlfriend answered a text message with the words, "Be well my friend." She knew that they were good friends; however, to receive the written greeting "my friend" had a profound effect on her. The greeting made her think that we refer to people as our friends all the time; yet somehow there is an additional comfort in knowing just how much of a friend we really are to someone.

My sister now makes it a point to include "my friend" or "my dear friend" in her messages. There is something touching about seeing and declaring friendship and kindness in writing!

"Dear friend, I pray that you may enjoy good health and that all may go well with you, even as your soul is getting along well."
—III John 1:2 (NIV)

Love everyone and everything with love and gratitude. Allow everyone to be just as they are and everything just as it is. Praise God for the perfection it all is. God believes in us; let us believe in each other's perfection. Have mercy on each other, trusting that we will all grow into our own greatness.

"Blessed are the merciful, for they shall **receive mercy.**"

—Matthew 5:7 (ESV)

Chapter 23

STEP 8: EXPECT THE MIRACLE IN EVERY MOMENT

The truth is, this whole life is miraculous. I write this humble book to bless humanity with a joyful reminder of how great our God is.

Along the way, we have come to believe that UPS, FedEx, and DHL can deliver faster than God. How did this happen? When did this happen? We have drifted so far away from the supernatural greatness of our mighty Universe.

If we order online and we click on express checkout, we expect the delivery to come the next day and we happily wait for our package at the front door with full confidence. How fast do we expect our delivery from the Ether, the most perfect delivery system of all time? It is up to us to recreate the expectation that miracles are available to us in every moment.

"Trust in the LORD with all your heart and lean not on your own understanding; in all your ways **submit to him**, and he will make your paths straight."
—Proverbs 3:5-6 (NIV)

Life is a series of choices. Let us choose to see everything as the miracle it is. In Christ all things are possible.

"Jesus looked at them and said, 'With man this is impossible, but with God **all things are possible.**'"
—Matthew 19:26 (NIV)

Step 8: Expect The Miracle In Every Moment

A dear friend of mine was very content being a single mother after her divorce; thus, she put little attention on dating. Her focus was on her career and raising her two beautiful children. She always said, "If a man wishes to date me, he will have to knock on my door."

Sure enough, about four years ago, one did knock on her door. A handsome man asked her what she was paying for her rent, because he owned a house five doors away that he wished to rent out. Soon after, he asked her out for dinner. Eventually they both moved from the neighborhood. They are still happily dating years later. The miracle came knocking.

When my husband and children went to the store to rent a movie, I went along and waited in the checkout area. As they were deciding on movies, I browsed through the magazine rack. I picked one up, opened it, and on that very page I saw a picture of two of my closest friends attending a ball. I took the magazine home and showed it to them. They were surprised that their picture was featured in the magazine, because after all it was a wedding magazine.

It was a most surprising place for my two single friends to be featured and more unique was for me to pick up a copy and browse through it. This miraculous finding also happened during another occasion when

I picked up a newspaper from my mail table. I again saw one of the same friends smiling at me from one of the pages.

If we choose to live our lives seeking and expecting miracles in our daily walk, we will recognize them everywhere.

Chapter 24

STEP 9: HAVE FUN AND CELEBRATE

Naturally, this last step is the most fun, yet honestly it does require our action.

As said in the Holy Bible, let us be like a child to enter into heaven. Life was given to us to live it abundantly, to celebrate with the heart of a child, and have fun. Let us enjoy our life experiences in a child-like state.

"And he said: 'Truly I tell you, unless you change and **become like little children,** you will never enter the kingdom of heaven.'"

—Matthew 18:3 (NIV)

Let us make sure that we remember to laugh like children all the time. Laughter inspires hope and forgiveness. The happier our attitude and the more we smile and laugh, the healthier our minds and bodies are. Laughter relaxes the whole body and releases tension.

Laughter and smiles increase "happy hormones" like endorphins, dopamine, and serotonin. Among other health benefits, it has been proven that the habit of laughing improves the function of our blood vessels, boosts the immune system, and also burns calories.

 Two big questions for most of us are:

First, can we remember what is fun for us?

Second, do we trust that God desires us to enjoy this lifetime and have fun?

 Take a moment right now to write a list of what is fun to you. List things that you already do and things that you wish to do to have more fun in your life.

Every day pick one suggestion and spend 15 minutes or more taking the action toward your goal of experiencing joy from your list and re-imagining your dreams.

Continually add to your list of fun. Please inspire us by sharing your fun ideas.

I collected some celebration ideas to share:

FUN IDEAS

- ♥ Have tea, meditate, light candles, sing, listen to your favorite music (inspirational, healing frequencies, island music, your good-mood songs)

- ♥ Do crafts like needle point, knitting, scrapbooking, jewelry

- ♥ Redecorate your home

- ♥ Create something with your hands: for example, an outdoor garden where you plant seeds and take pride in watching them grow, make fancy envelopes, an art journal, a vision board

- ♥ Write a book, create a picture book or mini books

- ♥ Spend time with family, go outside, or play games

- ♥ Play with your pets

♥ Connect with friends: go out, call them, or have them over at your place

♥ Buy flowers: smell them and notice their vivid colors and beauty

♥ Have fun with food: have an organic treat, bake cookies, cook something new, make popcorn the old-fashioned way in a pan, make a pizza from scratch

♥ Be active: take a walk or hike, dance through your house, jump on a trampoline, do your favorite exercise such as yoga, horseback riding, bowling, tennis, kayaking, swimming

♥ Be relaxed: enjoy a massage or a spa treatment of your choice

♥ Enjoy nature: mountains, beaches, forests, rivers, lakes, waterfalls, hot springs, salt grottos, islands; be mesmerized by crabs on the beach, watch the sunset with a picnic

♥ Shop or just meander through favorite stores: book stores, kitchen stores, office supply stores, paper craft stores

- ♥ Go on vacation, travel, go to a theme park, stay overnight in a hotel, take a city trip

- ♥ Learn something new, possibly a new language for your next trip

- ♥ Laugh from deep down in your belly until tears of joy come to your eyes, surround yourself with people with a good sense of humor or an ability to tell funny stories that make you laugh, share funny stories so other people laugh

- ♥ Have a fun photo shoot

- ♥ Actively belong to a community: church, gym, book club, Miracle Group, meditation circle, start your own group (for example, a movie group), and so on

- ♥ Manifest things

Step 9: Have Fun And Celebrate

Let us ask ourselves: How can we celebrate every day?

Let us create our own individual board game. If we create each space on our board of our Receive Joy game **Life of Fun**, then whatever number we roll with the dice is a winner. We can go forward or backward on the game board and we will always win something wonderful. If we write each fun card ourselves, then we are happy with every card in the deck.

When we pick up our pen to script our life and include everything that is fun, exciting to us, and satisfies our wildest dreams, then life is always a winning game.

"This is the day that the Lord has made; let us rejoice and be glad in it."
—Psalm 118:24 (ESV)

Let us live every moment in the present and ask ourselves how we can celebrate our life in this moment. There is only the present moment.

Let us allow ourselves to have fun. Most of us wait, rather than take action, to allow our dreams to come true. We hold off for the weekend, vacation, summer, retirement, special occasions, when we are older, when we have more time, when we feel better, or when we have the money. There is only now. Life is a series of now-moments. When we are six years old, it is now. When we are 20 years old, it is now. Now is now. Be here in the moment. Let us decide to live each perfect moment now.

Step 9: Have Fun And Celebrate

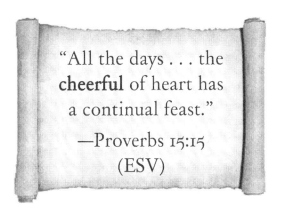

"All the days . . . the **cheerful** of heart has a continual feast."

—Proverbs 15:15 (ESV)

Let us also happily create for celebrations. When a close friend of my daughter turned 16, we chose to joyfully celebrate her birthday with a tea party. We decided to use a different cup and saucer for every girl attending. When we set the table, we were four saucer and cup combinations short. My daughter, who was throwing the party, said, "Mom, let us buy four more sets."

I asked her how much money she had to buy the four sets. She said, "I have $8 to spend, which means I have $1 for each cup and each saucer." My daughter and I love to go to thrift stores. We entered the Goodwill shop and walked directly to the shelf with the household items. The shelf was empty except for four elegant china teacups and saucers, each with a beautifully unique pattern. The teacups and saucers cost $1 each.

We still have the dainty sets and every time we use them they make us smile in memory of our creation power.

A further question is, "Can we rejoice?" Let us pick up the joy in our own life. Joy is always there. It is a stand-alone. It lies like a coin on our table. Let us pick it up, put it in our pocket and take it with us everywhere we go. Joy is also made up of one of the highest emotional vibrations. When we **feel good**, we are lifted into the flow of attraction.

"Rejoice in the Lord
always: and again
I say, Rejoice."
—Philippians 4:4
(KJV)

Let us rejoice always!

On a vacation to North Carolina, I took my youngest daughter out to the beach and she chased crabs with her little net. Whenever she approached the crabs, they quickly escaped. It was time for dinner and I told her that after dinner we will come back and catch a crab.

As we were walking back to the house, I said to God, "I am excited to see **how** you will make this happen. Wow me!" As promised, we went back to the beach after dinner. To our surprise, we found it full of crabs. Hundreds of them were absolutely mesmerized by the full moon and thus sitting out in the open and resting, completely different from earlier. My child caught lots of crabs.

We both rejoiced. I rejoiced as a mother, because I saw my child happy and my child rejoiced in her wish to catch crabs becoming a reality. For me, it was a miracle. I never saw so many crabs in my life. Sing praises to Him! Hymn Him!

Let us choose to have fun with our creations. Think outside the box. For example, let us talk to our bank accounts and tell them what we desire. Let us bless our food and ask it to give us the nutrition our body requires. Let us freeze our popsicles and ask one color to stay liquid. Let us ask our bushes to bloom in a different color this year. Let us have fun and be creative!

We may also use the Nine Steps to **enhance our entertainment factor** as one of my friends did while watching the Super Bowl: "A few years ago during the Super Bowl, the Seahawks had a 'first and goal' at the Patriots' five-yard line and they moved the ball closer without scoring.

"The clock ran under one minute and the Seahawks faced a 'second and goal' at the Patriots' one-yard line. This is when I wrote down on a piece of paper at my friend's house, 'Thank you, dear Jesus, for letting the Patriots intercept the ball.'

"The Patriots assumed the Seahawks may run the ball; instead they threw a pass and the Patriot's rookie Butler beat the Seahawk's player Lochette to the goal line and intercepted the pass. This was only possible with the help of the Patriots' most important player: Thank you again dear Jesus."

They surely had a fun Super Bowl celebration.

Use the Nine Steps to **create more fun along the way**. When two friends and I were backpacking over the Alps from Munich to Venice, we slept in mountain cabins with few food options. A small salad and pasta was our norm.

About three weeks into our journey, in the early afternoon, we were hungry again. My two friends and I were thinking about what kind of food appealed to us. In the morning, I said to one of my friends, "Since we are in Italy, I am craving homemade oven-baked pizza today." He agreed. When the discussion returned to food later in the day, our other friend, who had been absent from our morning conversation, added the same wish: Pizza. We all looked at each other and declared, "Let us have pizza."

We had fun imagining having a pizza restaurant on the mountain. Five minutes later, we came to a clearing and there it was: a pizza restaurant! We went running the rest of the way to the restaurant and enjoyed a fresh pizza from an Italian pizza oven as we sat in front of an open fire. I wish we had created more places along our journey like this.

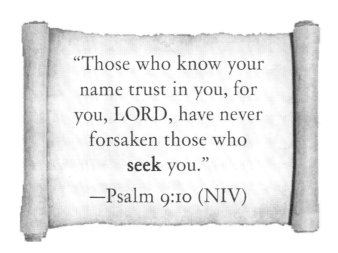

"Those who know your name trust in you, for you, LORD, have never forsaken those who **seek** you."

—Psalm 9:10 (NIV)

Part Three

Knock!

Chapter 25

THE POWER OF
CONSCIOUS PRACTICE

When using the Nine Step Method consciously on a daily basis, we are equipped to call in whatever we desire.

All the information is already contained in the seed. An apple seed contains all the information to mature into an apple tree.

We have everything that is essential for a fantastic life already preprogrammed in us. The great tree in all of us was already molded into us before we were born. Let us allow ourselves to grow organically. The more nurturing the conditions we plant the seed in, the faster, freer, and more sturdy the tree grows.

We can do this by keeping ourselves in a happy and nurturing environment. As with fertile soil, it is fruitful to keep our minds thinking positive and happy thoughts. Thus, we shall remain calm and relaxed and enjoy our creation.

If we guide our mind to think good thoughts, our mouth will share these good thoughts in the form of good words, and our deeds will follow in goodness. We are complete. Let us listen to our inner guidance system.

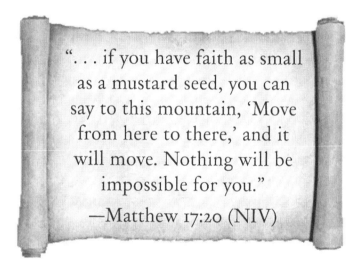

"... if you have faith as small as a mustard seed, you can say to this mountain, 'Move from here to there,' and it will move. Nothing will be impossible for you."
—Matthew 17:20 (NIV)

God is in charge of the seed planted in us, and therefore the kind of plant into which we mature. Our influence is on the branches and leaves we grow from the stem and the environment we choose to place ourselves in.

Let us choose to have strong and nurturing branches. Let us surround ourselves with nurturing soil and an environment to grow branches that weather all storms and allow birds to rest in its shade.

> "It is like a mustard seed, which is the smallest of all seeds on earth. Yet when planted, it grows and becomes the largest of all garden plants, with such big branches that the birds can perch in its shade."
>
> —Mark 4:31-32 (NIV)

Let us create the desire and the time to apply the Nine Steps. Throughout the book there are games and exercises to build your creation power. Life is about having fun and collecting experiences.

> "I came that they may **have life**, and have it **abundantly**."
>
> —John 10:10 (ESV)

Here are three simple **Receive Joy Games** for you to joyfully exercise your creation muscle.

FIVE MINUTE COUCH TIME

The Five Minute Couch Time is time that we designate to be with our inner self and God. It is a time when only I am important and the world is on hold. Let us use our Five Minute Couch Time to:

♥ Ponder a question we wish to solve: "God please show me a way to accomplish this."

♥ Restate our question to receive a better answer: "What I really mean is . . .".

For example, a year ago, I took a Five Minute Couch Time and formed the thought of writing a book about my life's enlightened understanding of the Quantum World. I know that I love myself so much that I deserve someone to come stay with me and support me in the venture of writing this book. I went through the parameters I set up for this person to fulfill:

1. This co-author is willing to live at my house full time to work with me.

2. We share the same desires and values.

---

3. This co-author has a developed under-standing and training in Quantum Physics.

4. The writing process will be light and easy because of this collaboration.

5. I love this person and our ideas continu-ously complement each other's.

6. My co-creator is computer-savvy and organized.

Last May, during a European vacation with my family, we met our former intern from Germany who had stayed with us on and off for four years whenever she had a break from her study of business psychology. When we asked her what her future plans were, she answered, "I am happy and content with all the years of traveling around the world on various cruise ships, cargo ships, and yachts, and now I am ready to write a book."

It all fell into place very easily as the Universe shook us out, matched us with our desires, and aligned us (once again) to begin this amazing journey we are on. As you read through this book, you will notice that it is written in the singular although it is in fact powered by two creative minds. We are Rece & Ive Joy.

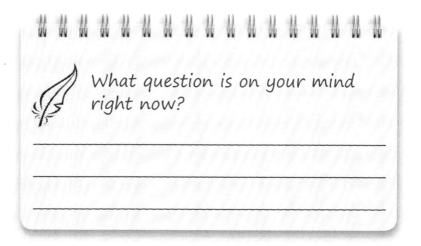

What question is on your mind right now?

_____

_____

_____

TEN STAR EXPERIENCE

Let us make every experience a Ten Star Experience.

Let us set parameters and define what it will take to make an experience even more fun. What will it take to make each experience in our day a Ten Star Experience? Let us grab our journals and write down five to 10 ideas to raise the bar of fun.

I love grocery shopping even more when . . .

♥ I bring my shopping list.

♥ I bring a friend.

- ♥ I bring my reusable bags.

- ♥ I bring a jacket (in most stores it is cold inside).

- ♥ I wear comfortable shoes.

- ♥ I bring lots of money.

- ♥ I smile and greet everyone.

- ♥ I find a recipe that I am excited to try featuring the vegetable of the season.

- ♥ I buy something new. For example, a fruit or a vegetable I am curious about and I find a recipe to use it in.

- ♥ I leave my cart at the end of an isle and walk up and down to collect my items while receiving exercise.

I love exercise even more when . . .

- ♥ I choose an activity that is fun for me, like yoga.

- ♥ I have clothes that feel comfortable and are right for the occasion and the weather.

- ♥ I bring water with me.

♥ I bring a friend.

♥ I schedule exercise appointments with myself on my calendar.

♥ I treat myself to the exercise session.

♥ I try out something new, a new pose in yoga or a fun sport.

♥ I schedule treats for myself. I treat myself to a massage after two weeks of exercising three times per week.

What experience do you wish to enhance right now?

_____

_____

_____

CREATE A SUPERNATURAL SHIP

All of us require a space in which we can be comfortable and relax in peace. A **floating workshop** is a place in our minds and hearts where we can always go to relax and enjoy. Here, there is only a place for our "self". Here, everything is perfect.

I like to imagine that each of us has such a place in the form of a **Supernatural Ship**, which floats above the Earth and hovers steadily over our life. It is a place where we have a heavenly perspective from which we look down on our life and our loved ones. On this platform, we have both hands on the steering wheel to maneuver wherever we wish to be and we have a comforting place just for our "self".

Do you have such a ship? Let us start from the very beginning and build our own ship.

First, write a list of beautiful words or use the one you have written earlier. Each positive word is a board that we nail to others to make a platform strong enough to hold us.

What do we require to hold our ship together? Let us use every single word we wrote on our beautiful word list. Visualize each word as a strong board.

As they are bound together, they now form a Supernatural Ship that we can stand and rest on.

Place the boards in your mind and heart to create stability to feel good all the time. Absorb all the positive words; have them embrace your inner being.

Ask yourself: What serves me on my life's platform? What is it I desire on my ship? Keep adding your positive words to make this platform bigger and more stable. Let it become your workshop.

Develop your customized space. What does it look like? Is it comfortable, peaceful, and quiet? Is it lined with soft pillows?

If your gut is tense, ask yourself: Which boards are missing on my ship? What can be added to make it strong enough to hold me? Is it "faith" or "honesty"? Are there any holes? Is the ship big enough? Is every board big enough? Do I have all the boards that are important to me? Go through your list of positive words over and over and put the missing boards in the right places.

If earthly matters seem to overtake us and we jump off our ship and are floating around, is there even a ship to climb back on? Can we climb back on easily? How long does it take us to climb back on? Can we still visualize our ship?

Can we stay in joy, even when a challenge enters our lives? A stable ship can create an environment that leaves us in peace and with the ability to function even before, amidst, and after a challenge arises. We can be in control. Do we have the most important board attached? In Christ all things are possible. God is always here. This platform is our safe haven.

Let us declare that this is our own ship. When someone is floating around us, we can make the decision, if we are rightminded enough, to help that person. Let us keep both hands on the wheel. We can invite others to sit on our deck for a while, to dry off and

rest from their storm. We can encourage them enough to be able to climb back on their own ship. Truthfully, let us remain the only soul entering our private comfort zone.

When we man our own ship, we can pull our perfect ship alongside other rightminded ships to create a stable platform for ourselves and others to celebrate life. We are most helpful to each other when everyone has their own hands and attention on their own steering wheel. Let us make conscious decisions about whom we wish to sail alongside in this life as we maintain our balance and comfort.

Maybe some people still desire a ship of their own and jump from one ship to another. Some ships are barely afloat. Some people, upon examining their life, might realize that they have holes in most of their boards.

This life is given to each of us to investigate our own "self" and choose to bring glory. Continue to joyfully build your Supernatural Ship. Take a Five Minute Couch Time each day to strengthen your boards and do maintenance on your ship. Ask yourself what felt good about today and what you may plan to create differently next time.

Chapter 26

THE POWER OF PRAYER

Pray often. Let us pray as we wake up, over our meals, before we go to bed, and often throughout the day. Prayers are our intentions offered to God. Since we are focusing on the positive, pray with a rejoicing heart and thanksgiving. Pray into the solution. Ask for the solution as if it is already granted. Use positive words and be in a positive mindset. The vibration of prayer is strong.

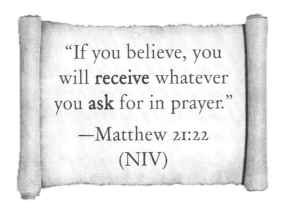

"If you believe, you will **receive** whatever you **ask** for in prayer."

—Matthew 21:22 (NIV)

When searching the Internet, there are numerous stories of "healing through prayer". Just to give one example, in a hospital in China the staff uses prayer on inoperable cancer patients. Doctors from the hospital gather in the patient's room and pray. At the same time, the lobby is full of people praying for the patient. While they are praying, they use ultrasound to show the mass shrinking in real time.

We have all heard many stories in which prayer has miraculously healed, helped, and comforted. So many people received peace, abundance, and happiness through it. Prayer allows the physical manifestation of the Power of God.

To pray and cheer for ourselves each day, let us use these positive words of a simple yet powerful prayer and see our lives transform. This is based on the prayer found in the Holy Bible when Jabez called on God in I Chronicles 4:10.

> "Dear God, bless me,
> increase my territory,
> wrap your arms around me,
> and keep me in your righteous arena."

The Power Of Prayer

There is a mechanism in the Universe that answers to **the Power of Agreement between two or more parties**:

> "Again I say to you, if **two** of you **agree** on earth about anything they ask, it will be done for them by my Father in heaven. For where two or three gather in my name, there am I with them."
>
> —Matthew 18:19-20 (NIV)

This Power of Agreement is similar to a 1.5-volt battery combined with another 1.5-volt battery. When they are linked together, they become more powerful than the individual alone. When a flashlight requires two batteries, the light only turns on when both are in place.

The Universe is set up in a way that when two or more individuals come together, the light begins to shine even brighter and miracles happen. Quantum Physics supports Aristotle's theory, "The whole is more than the sum of its parts."

This is how the board meetings of large companies are run to set their goals. One person introduces an idea or a motion and another member of the board seconds the motion. The administrative assistant writes it down and the motion is passed.

Similarly, we have this ability to create with the agreeing force of another individual. The other person can participate in agreement and encouragement of our set goals even when the other person is only slightly aware of the content. We can "high five" each other or have the other person initial our written statement, speak about it, or partake in whatever method we feel comfortable with.

My two sisters make it a ritual of calling each other every Monday morning. They go through their lists of what they desire to call in for the week encompassing all areas of their lives. After they **second the motion** for everything they each wish to attract, **they pray over it**.

For over three years now this ritual has become their safe haven and the most important appointment of the week. Many miraculous stories were created with this focused discipline.

Let us form Prayer Alliances or Miracle Groups with friends and family.

During our family trip in Alaska, I took my then six-year-old daughter whale watching. Once we were heading out in the boat, my daughter said to me, "Mom, I am kind of bored. We better see a whale." **I agreed with her** and calmly and confidently verbally assured her "we will see a whale". At that very moment, a huge whale breached right in front of the boat just 30 feet away.

When one of my clients visited me, it was obvious that he was challenged. I asked him what brought this on and what he desired to change in order for him to become calmer.

His business is buying and restoring houses. Usually, he had a maximum of one or two houses. Currently he had three houses. To be more calm, he desired to sell two of the houses.

We immediately declared that two houses were sold. He called me the next evening and reported that two houses sold during the day. We matched our agreements in request and the Universe answered us.

This is why Jesus gathered His disciples. Whether people go to seminars, concerts, live sport events, or gather in church and pray on Sundays, they are all sharing the elevated vibrational energy of the group. When we pray in a group, we enhance our focus and desires.

A friend of mine who works at a casino told me that for Christmas one year, the general manager gave every employee a copy of the book *The Secret* along with their bonus check. He asked his employees what improvement they might pursue to bring in new revenue for the casino. They all came up with fabulous ideas and they voted on attaching a hotel to the casino.

When she told me the story, I asked her, "Is there currently a hotel attached?" To her own surprise she said, "By golly, yes, there is." Let us realize how many things we create daily that come true.

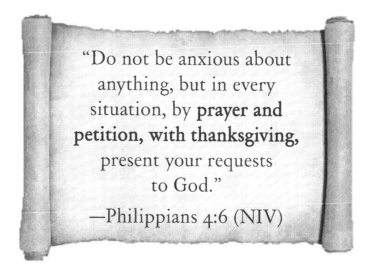

"Do not be anxious about anything, but in every situation, by **prayer and petition, with thanksgiving,** present your requests to God."
—Philippians 4:6 (NIV)

In addition to declaring our goals, we can assist others with their desires.

The Power Of Prayer

A client of mine used the Power of Attraction in his then 10-year-old daughter's life. The girl loved fast food and wished to improve in academics. He was concerned about her weight gain and wished to create a way to motivate her. He desired his daughter to participate in track and field.

Before he talked to her, he decided to do his research by going to her school and talking with her teachers. He wished to know what interested her besides watching TV and eating fast food. What he found out came as a big surprise to him: His daughter practiced shot put on the playground during break. Since she was sturdier than other kids her age, she excelled at this sport. She constantly begged the coach to allow her to participate in afterschool practice. The coach encouraged her to improve her academic scores in order to join the team.

Her dad then came up with a great idea to motivate her: for every improvement in her grades, he gave her money to spend on her beloved fast food. He also gave her $10 in advance to show her his serious commitment. Shortly thereafter, her grades improved and her overall academic scores allowed her to join the team. She was even selected to participate in the primary championships representing her school.

Now she is fourteen, in perfect health and weight, and continues to take part in competitions. Let us help each other to focus our intentions and share in the asking.

Over the years, a friend of mine asked me to be her prayer partner for her family's happiness and well-being. We prayed for a wonderful husband for her daughter and he appeared. We asked for two healthy grandchildren for her and she was blessed with them also. One brilliant aspect of this alliance is, along with asking for ourselves, we can also ask for those we love.

Healthy habits and lives were asked for loved ones and now that wish has been fulfilled. What a gift we can give to ourselves and others any time, any place! It is free. Let us pray with sincere declaration, focused thought, loving words, and a pen to write it down.

Jesus healed a Roman centurion's servant simply because the Roman asked Jesus for help (Luke 7:1-10).

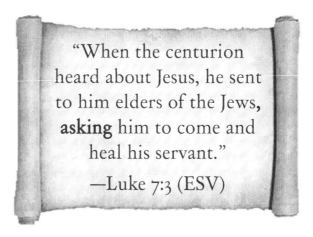

"When the centurion heard about Jesus, he sent to him elders of the Jews, **asking** him to come and heal his servant."

—Luke 7:3 (ESV)

The Power Of Prayer

The following prayer is our Miracle Group prayer. Let us pray together!

Dear Father God,

You are the light of my life.
Thank You for this perfect day. Thank You for this perfect moment.

Thank You for creating me in Your image.
I accept that I am Your child and that I hold Your creation power.

Thank You for Your wisdom.
Thank You for allowing me plenty of time to accomplish everything.
Most of all, I am thankful that You are always with me and are my greatest support.

My life is balanced and flows light and easy.
I recognize the good that is abundant everywhere.

I am calm. I have a peaceful heart.

I am Love.

I love myself so that I can have love for others.
I find it easy to love myself and others.
Love flows through me and touches everyone in my life.
My love is so great that it surrounds all and everything.

I constantly create great thoughts of love and joy.
I am Joy. I am a true blessing.
Keep me cheerful so that I may serve You.

I am grateful that I know the truth.
I am grateful that I have a definite life's purpose.

I am grateful that I use beautiful words that create.
I am grateful for my perfect health. I am beautiful.

I am grateful that I am incredibly successful and that wealth and abundance come from everywhere. Money flows frequently and abundantly.

I rejoice in You Jesus.

With love, gratitude, and happiness,

Your loving child

Chapter 27

THE POWER OF MIRACLE GROUPS

A few years ago, a group of friends decided to come together and practice positive intentions. During our meetings we share positive words and energy, we learn, listen, and refine our manifesting skills. We are likeminded individuals who help and encourage each other, second our motions, and have open-minded conversations. We let each other know our desires for what we are wishing to receive through the habit of manifestation, and then in the following meetings we share our manifested miracles while encouraging each other with great love and gratitude. We practice collective intention in harmony with other energetic positive minds.

The Power Of Miracle Groups

We meet every two weeks for most of the year and these meetings have become a place for meaningful friendships, support, inspirations, respect, love, acceptance of all, reminders, joy, and rediscovering the truth. This is our Miracle Group. We embrace with optimism that we are part of a larger whole.

Many of the stories in this book are manifestations from the Miracle Group.

Here are some words members of the Miracle Group used to describe their experiences:

"I love listening to the wonderful new miracles that everyone shares at each meeting. The support of seconding each other's prayer requests is important to me. I also look forward to the joy of just seeing each other and listening to all the joyous, happy, beautiful words every two weeks."

"When a friend mentioned to me she was in the Miracle Group, it excited me and I said, 'Oh, can I come too?' She said, 'Sure.' I was curious to know what it was all about since it related to manifesting. They were all strangers except for one friend and the group leader.

"Within a few short weeks, we were forming new friendships. We love God and care about each other. We support each other. We use positive words with each other. We have bonded and love each other. We are all fortified when we hear about the manifestations of others.

"Meeting every two weeks is a good reminder to stay positive and to know that if this works for others it will also work for me. It is a very good feeling to be with others who think the same way I do."

"When I moved to town, I asked everyone I met if they knew of people who were likeminded. Soon, I met a woman who was a member of the Miracle Group. This group makes me realize how simple life is. We co-create our own lives with God. In our group we help, encourage, and excite each other. We spend time in our meetings having fun with one another.

"This group encourages me to organize my words and thoughts better. It is great when we envision our days and our lives as we wish them to be. Positive mindset and energy is so encouraging and happy experiences follow. I feel so great and grateful for each wonderful person in the group. This amazing time inspires us to live positive lives."

"I am a member of the Miracle Group in which we all practice positive words and conscious thinking. I successfully use the Nine Steps. Now I understand that I am able to ask by declaring as if it already happened and things will come true. I learned that if I write my desired outcome just once it will manifest with God's help.

"Another relearning has been the use of positive words. Many times I play golf and tennis with people who, after only small mistakes with their games, feel compelled to announce that today they 'cannot' putt or hit a backhand. Their subconscious soon follows and fulfills their words and the behavior matches.

"This makes my game a lot easier. I told one lady I will charge her for each negative word she uttered about herself. Happily, she changed her tune, became more positive about herself, and now is a more self-assured golfer.

"Now I have learned the language of God's miraculous Universe. The Nine Steps Method can be embraced by all who choose to declare in writing what they are asking for. Thus, marvelous outcomes can be received. Who knew? Now I do!"

One day, when the Miracle Group was meeting, a member felt sorry for herself. Instead of attending the group to be together with all her friends, she was lying in bed with her clothes on, going back to her old scheme, and feeling the absence of self-empowerment.

Since she told me earlier in the day that she will be attending the meeting, I called her 10 minutes after the meeting began and asked, "Where are you?" She lived across the street from the meeting. She stood up, washed her face, and came over to be around friends.

The meeting refocused her mind on the joy in her life. Times like this are when we cherish the Miracle Group most.

If you wish to have your own Miracle Group, we are happy to help supply topics for the meetings. Please contact us by email.

Chapter 28

THE POWER OF JOURNALING

Journaling enhances our conscious creating power. In order to advance our lives, let us write into the solution.

First, we journal our goals, then we keep score by journaling our achievements. Whenever we have received answers to our prayers, we write them down to have a fantastic record of all we have gained. This helps us build our confidence and develops our creation muscle. All the stories in this book have been journaled at one point.

Let us use the time in the evening before we go to bed to reflect on our day and recall everything we did or people we met who brought us closer to our goals. This serves to show us that we are in control of our choices, our creations, and our growth.

Journaling also helps us to focus on more details. When we consciously recognize what we receive, we apply the Nine Steps more eagerly. The more consciously we attract, the better life becomes.

For example, when we start our own business or charity, we start meeting the perfect people to help us with our vision. We will attract referrals and professionals who are able to design our logo and business cards. Another contact we meet may have the ability to set up our webpage and so forth. When we focus on a location for our business, we might drive by a building, which will excellently serve our vision.

As our mission becomes more and more defined, we joyfully take the time to write down what we attracted during the day and how our business and other goals are shaping up beautifully. This is also a good time to be grateful for what we already accomplished. At the same time, let us state what we wish to attract for the next day and the next week and everything that we fancy to reach our goals perfectly. Once we have written down everything we desire, let us pray over it.

Make a priority of journaling. Let us write down our words to bring them into this physical dimension and give form to our creation. Read over them and **edit yourself three times** to make sure all words are positive and are a blessing. There is great power in the pen. Revisit the editing suggestions in Part One till they are a familiar habit.

Thank goodness, Jesus inspired people to write things down on scrolls. Thus, we now have the Word of the Lord, *"The Holy Bible"*: our manual to this life's experience.

A friend owed the bank $250,000 for his second mortgage. The bill collector called him and asked him how much he was able to pay. "I am about to receive an $8,000 check from an insurance claim. I can offer you that $8,000 to satisfy the debt." The bill collector replied, "This is a very low offer. I have yet to see the bank accept such a low offer."

He calmly told the man, "Write my offer down on paper and please forward the offer to the bank. Then, post the paper on your wall and see the creation power of the written word."

Two weeks later, the bill collector called again and said that the bank agreed on his suggested settlement offer. My friend happily replied to the bill collector, "Remember when I told you to write it down and post it on your wall? Now you know how I create everything!" He hung up the phone and gave thanks to Jesus.

It also helps when we divide our journal or notebook into sections by using tab dividers. Then we can find the section right away to easily write down what we attract and wish for throughout the day. Ideas for the sections are:

♥ **Divine Purpose**: To write our Mission Statement/Life's Purpose

♥ **Miracles**: To list all the orders we wish to attract

♥ **Gains Received**: To keep score of that which we consciously created

♥ **Fun**: To list everything that is fun for us

♥ **Beautiful Words**: To collect all beautiful words and phrases that inspire

♥ **Gratitude**: To list everyone and everything we are grateful for

♥ **Heaven**: To describe what our ideal life looks like

♥ **Family & Friends**: To order for others

♥ **Notes**: To gather new ideas, tape in sticky notes, words, pictures, and images that inspire us

The Power Of Journaling

We call this journal our **Receive Joy Journal**.

Our journal also serves us whenever we create something unique. I go back in my journal to find out where and when I created it.

Some time ago, I was asking myself why I have two jet skis in my second garage. I went through my journals and had to go back 17 years to find when I ordered them. I wrote down, "I have jet skis." Here they are. I see I ordered them.

Let us take the time to write down our desires. Create a moment—make time! Declare to yourself, "I have all the time in the world to support myself." Affirm what is important in your life each day. This process is fundamental for a successful life. Here are some ideas on how I started:

♥ Before going to bed—I am thankful for the day and map out my next day. I write five things I wish to see accomplished for the next day on a sticky note and pray over it.

♥ Upon arising—I have Breakfast with God and go through my sticky note of five things I wish to accomplish today.

♥ Whenever a new situation in the day arises, I take a few minutes and ask myself the question, "What can I welcome in to make this experience a Ten Star Experience"?

♥ When I have a situation to ponder, I take a Five Minute Couch Time break.

♥ I use the time in the restaurant with my family and friends to ask everyone to write down their desires, between ordering food and receiving it. It also helps when we visualize and verbalize our written goals during the process.

♥ When I recognize a creation, I write it in the Gains Received section of my journal.

♥ I pass it on. I share my goals, gains, and desires to encourage myself and others.

While my girlfriend and I were writing our goals, we wrote, "Since the children now have a dog to walk, they may also have a dog walking business." When we went downstairs, the girls brought home three neighborhood dogs with them. They explained to us that they now have a dog walking business.

They made $700 the first year and $1,500 the

second year. They were six, eight, and nine years old at that time. Still today, my children help in the neighborhood. They are 15, 17, and 19 years old and continue to walk dogs, water plants, house-watch, and babysit as they actively share joy and help others.

Start journaling!

Chapter 29

THE POWER OF MEDITATION

Let us ask ourselves: Is our cup half full or is it running over? How do we fill it up? The only way the cup can fill up is with a continual pouring in of joy, gratitude, appreciation, happiness, awareness, consciousness, praise, calmness, peace, and love for ourselves and others.

Meditation is a quiet time we spend with our inner self. Let us consciously choose to make time and just be. 15 minutes a day is all it takes. Sitting or lying in a peaceful, comfortable place allows us to focus on our breathing, which relaxes the body. After we are calm and relaxed, be conscious and honor the first thought you receive in this state. The first thought our subconscious sends us is our inspired thought.

The Power Of Meditation

Let us clear our minds and open our awareness for our cup of life to refill continuously.

To help fill you up, we created an Ask And You Shall Receive Meditation using only positive words. For your convenience and delight, this Receive Joy Meditation is available on CD. Please listen to it as often as you like to master your thoughts, to feel good, practice the Nine Steps, and to remain in perfect health. It shall:

♥ Help you to harness your peaceful energy and call in your abundance.

♥ Bring you continual happiness and calmness.

♥ Help your inner being to see the truth and trust in the Almighty Power to see clear opportunities and create only good things in your life.

♥ Help you stay in tune with your power and enable you to live in your friendly world all the time.

♥ Reset yourself to the divine perfection that you already are.

These are the words of the Ask And You Shall Receive Meditation. I chose each word in prayer, blessing, and joy.

I am comfortable. My mind is at peace. I am calm. My mind is wide open. I have a peaceful heart. I am relaxed.

I choose to focus only on my breath. I take three deep breaths. Inhale deeply. Exhale fully. Inhale deeply. Exhale fully. Inhale deeply. Exhale fully.

As I look up into the sky, I see the heavens. I feel connected to a power that is greater than my individual self. I know that this is the power that I come from. It surrounds me. This is light.

This source of light is God's Almighty Power. This beautiful, continual, abundant power. It is formulated from love. It is light and life. It is warm. It is comforting. It is here to support and comfort me. It embraces me. I know the light is here to love and support me. I know the light is here to help and comfort me. It is awesome and full of power.

This Almighty Power is abundant. It is free and equally available to everyone.

I recognize abundance everywhere. The Universe pulls from all resources of all existence. I understand the Almighty Power. I tap into all the abundance. I am so grateful that I am part of the wonderful, great abundance that all humanity comes from. I choose to connect to this power.

I can see this beautiful, powerful light over my head. It looks perfect. This beautiful light is abundant. I welcome this beautiful, perfect light. This beautiful light is the Almighty Power coming through me. It enters into the crown of my head and as it makes its way through my body, I relax even more.

I am calmer and calmer. I am perfect. I am the child of God. I am created in His image. I hold His creation power. I know His mercy. I hold His wisdom. I tap into His free gift of abundance and create my perfect life every day.

The light fills me. I am fulfilled. As it comes into the crown of my head, it balances my brain. It helps to focus my mind and my thoughts. I think positive thoughts that attract what I desire. I use the enormous power of my mind. I have the power to welcome only the thoughts that bless me. I have the power to turn away all opposing thoughts. I constantly create great thoughts of love and joy.

I know that what I focus on I receive more of. I am completely focused. By faith, I declare all my actions before I take them. With grace, I visualize the outcome. I declare the exact outcome. I reach my desires fast and accurately. I write great plans for my life. I am clear about what I intend for each day. I write down what I welcome in each day. I ask for my desires with great precision. I love to declare in exact detail.

I speak only beautiful words that create

and bless. I know every word counts. I stay completely focused. My beautiful words, my intended thoughts, and my written declarations set my path every day. I am the author of my life. I understand that my life's path is up to me.

The light helps to guide me. It gives me a clear vision. It allows me to smell the abundance. It helps me choose my words. It helps me to hear the voice of God. I understand that I am in co-creation with God. I know my inheritance is there for me to use and do great things with it. God gave me dominion over this Earth. I am a winner.

After I have declared my desires, I know the Universe is combining and processing my orders. I am a child of God.

The light travels down from my head. Now my neck moves easily. It reaches my shoulders. My shoulders sink down. I am more and more relaxed. All movement is free and easy. My arms are light. My arms are relaxed. My elbows are relaxed. My hands are open and at peace. I feel a tingle of joy in my fingertips. The light flows freely through my head, neck, shoulders, and down my arms into my hands.

I am completely calm. I have faith, I believe. My heart is at peace. My head is aligned with my heart. The light continues to travel down from my head through my spine. Every vertebrae is filled with light. My vertebrae are moving smoothly, they are flexible and aligned. The light fills my lungs.

I pay attention to my breath. I inhale deeply. I exhale fully. I am aware of my breath. The light stays with me and continues to nourish all my cells. The light covers my skin.

I am beautiful. I am amazed how beautiful I am. My skin glows. I have full, thick, and healthy hair. My cells are happy and well. My bones are firm yet flexible. My eyes see the glory of God. My mouth smiles and speaks blessings. My nose smells the beauty of nature. My ears hear the voice of the great I Am.

My body is perfectly healthy. My mind is perfectly balanced. My body is fit. I love my body. I exercise regularly. Exercise is so much fun. Being active brings me joy. I am active throughout the day. I stand up and walk around often.

I am in perfect health. I love to drink water.

I understand that water is the source of life and I can imprint it with loving and beautiful messages. I understand that I am made of water. Water serves me and I cherish it.

The warm light floods my chest and heart area. My blood is clean and flows perfectly. My heart loves continuously. I love myself. I am filled with love and gratitude. I love myself so that I can love others. I find it easy to love myself and others. I have a love for all humanity. I have great appreciation for everyone and everything in my life. Love flows through me and touches everyone in my life. My love is so great that it surrounds all and everything. Because I come from love, I am love.

The light travels through my whole body and every cell is glowing with light. It surrounds all my inner organs. I know what I desire. I choose to only focus on the positive things I am creating. I focus on the good in every moment. I see only the good in myself and others.

I am wealthy. As the light fulfills me, I think of all the wealth in my life: I am loving, kind, helpful, nurturing, and supportive. My family and friends are loving, kind, helpful, nurturing, and supportive. I enjoy spending time with myself and others. I have plenty of time. I attract money.

As the light reaches my lower body, it flows through my legs to my knees. My knees are relaxed. The light travels down my legs to my toes and leaves a tingling sensation of joy in my toes. I have happy feet.

I am successful. I continuously attract more success and fulfillment.

As the light is in me and surrounds my whole being, I am clear. My mind is genius. I have a perfect memory. I use my perfect memory to serve me. I remember whatever I wish to recall. I have all the information I desire. I am the information. I am wisdom. I know this is the truth.

The light travels to my solar plexus. I am in control of my emotions. My emotions serve me well. As I feel this light, I also feel the calmness it brings with it. My life is balanced and flows light and easy. I am at peace. I am calm. I am the sunshine of my life. I trust myself. I deserve everything that brings me joy. I am worthy. I am the child of the most high God. I understand the power of prayer, affirmation, and visualization. I know everything I focus on I receive more of. I believe in the absolute Power of God.

I have plenty of time to do whatever makes me happy. I receive everything I desire immediately.

I know the truth. I am grateful that I know my life's purpose. I live my life's purpose. I am happy and I am living the life of my dreams.

I take a moment to visualize my perfect life. I can see my perfect life. I visualize myself achieving all of my goals. I visualize my perfect life. I am living my perfect life.

Now I see before me my beautiful, happy life. I enter into my perfect creation.

I expect great things to continually come my way. My perfect life is full of abundance. It is full of peaceful energy. My world is friendly. My life is light and easy. I allow all that is good in and it flows joyfully. I have all the resources I require. I am resourceful.

I rejoice always. And again, I say rejoice. I am glad and rejoice in all. I understand that this life was given to me to be joyful and to celebrate. Thank you Jesus.

I am full of energy. I am happy and active. I have the energy of a child. My day is all planned out the night before. I am ready to live my day. I know my next step. I am aware of my creation power. I have all the resources. I am resourceful.

I choose to bring joy into every situation of my life. I make sure I am having fun every day. I always have joyful thoughts of harmony. I smile constantly. I think only great thoughts. I use only blessed words. I know every word counts.

I am grateful for this perfect day. I am grateful for every perfect moment. I live in the now. And I celebrate. The light calls out my inner being. The light dances with my inner being. The light embraces my inner being. I am so happy. I am joy. I feel the happiness now.

I am a true blessing. I am cheerful. I am fulfilled. I continuously call on my manifesting abilities throughout the day. As I go through my day, I use my creation power. The beautiful light stays with me throughout my day. Life is easy. I celebrate. It is easier day by day. I live my life to the fullest. I am well all the time. I have fun. I am a rejoicing soul. I rejoice in You Jesus. I am the light. I AM the light.

 Feel free to use these words and phrases throughout your daily walk and in front of your mirror. Use them as daily affirming inspiration.

Chapter 30

THE POWER OF VISUALIZATION

Visualization is the forming of visual images in our minds. Our brain thinks in pictures. Let us bring our desired images to our awareness throughout the day. When we enter a new situation, let us envision the desired outcome. What do we wish ourselves to say or do in order to serve our goals?

Daydreaming is another way of visualizing. Let us make time for daily meditation where we consciously create our perfect life in our mind. Let us paint a detailed picture in vivid color. When we **see our "self" in our desired life**, our mind believes that it is already here and looks for clues in reality to match our goals. Like attracts like.

The outer world and the inner world, or the so-called reality and a vividly imagined visualization, are both perceived as the same by the brain. When the brain is stimulated either way, the same areas of the brain are active with the same intensity. This is proven in studies using electroencephalogram or functional magnetic resonance imaging. What the mind believes to be true becomes our reality.

Everything starts from an idea. Visualizing our desires also increases our focus. Visualization has become an important training tool for athletes. There are numerous studies showing that the performance level significantly increases when the physical training is combined with visualization.

To further help our subconscious mind focus on our desires, let us create a **vision board**. I enjoy the habit of creating one for every new segment of my life. We can choose each New Year or a special event in the year to create one.

Now is the perfect time. Let us keep expanding our board as we go through our daily lives, collecting pictures and affirmations that serve us. The following story is about how a vision board changed my friend's life:

"In early January 1998, I joined a workshop on vision board preparation for the New Year. There was a brief discussion on setting our intentions, then the 10 of us were directed to the large table full of colorful magazine clippings showing fashion, cars, boats, various environments, and so on. We each had a big, white poster board, scissors, and glue and were instructed to randomly select the images that attracted our attention. Then we found a spot on the floor and began.

"As I arranged the images I had selected, I was aware that many of my chosen pictures featured water: water craft on a beautiful blue sea, ocean dunes with a couple watching the sunset, a family walking the beach, a seaside home with a pool overlooking the water.

"Then I chose a picture of an elegant woman with red lacquered nails and a large tanzanite stone surrounded by diamonds on her ring finger. I placed this picture in the middle of my board and surrounded it with the water themes.

"Since the front of the board was full, the only place for a large page of desert rock formations was on the back of the vision board. This picture made it into my pile, because it was very interesting and pleasing to my eyes.

"At the time, I had a successful insurance agency in Houston, Texas. I wished to expand beyond corporate politics and management. Two months after the workshop for vision board creation, my husband asked me if I fancied living on the water.

His friend and former manager was putting together a new group of investment bankers for a firm in St. Petersburg, Florida, and my husband was invited to join them. What an amazing opportunity.

"My husband was happily surprised that I answered yes immediately. I had an upcoming appointment with my new manager to review my business plans for the year. This meeting was a perfect opportunity to offer my 'retirement letter.'

"In January 1999 we sold our Houston home and we visited our favorite jewelry store for some farewell goodies with our two daughters. The four of us each received new watches. It was also my birthday and my husband picked out and bought me a beautiful diamond-and-tanzanite ring. And yes, it did look just like the ring in the picture on my vision board.

"We also bought a home on Tampa Bay with a pool and a dock. We enjoyed beautiful sunrises poolside and walked the nearby beaches regularly.

"And what about the picture on the reverse side of the vision board? It is now the view that I see each morning on my walks after our move to New Mexico in 2009. Currently, I am thinking it may be time for a new vision board."

Let us start collecting positive words, pictures, beautiful color patterns, and affirmations from magazines and from all around us. If a vision board is too big for your liking, tape the pictures in your Receive Joy Journal.

There are plenty of other fun opportunities for which they can also be used. We can liven up our lives with creative sayings and pictures. For example, my daughters surround themselves in their rooms with positive, uplifting art and sayings on their walls, doors, ceilings, furniture, and mirrors.

In my Miracle Group, the ladies are very creative. One is creating a **cover for every notebook** she uses from the scrap pieces she collects. It is a great inspiration to have beauty and positivity looking back at us from everywhere.

Another lady from my group does **art journaling**. She uses a fresh notebook every year. Along with the collected scraps, she also writes stories about her experiences and prayers for herself and others. She lists all she has already gained in her life and all the possibilities still open for her to experience. It is greatly encouraging to look back on our year and see the miracles we have experienced.

Sticky notes are also a great way to visualize. Write a different desire on each sticky note, then place them in a location we view every day to remind us of our desires.

The Power Of Visualization

The most brilliant location we found was the back of our bedroom door. This way it is easy to remove the goals already accomplished, add the new ones, and sort them by priority.

Around the dinner table of a Miracle Group meeting, we each received a pack of sticky notes to play a **game of Ask And You Shall Receive.** The rule of this game was that we had 10 minutes to fill all the pages of the pack with our desires.

Before dinner was served, we wrote one desire per page. During dinner, we all shared what we wrote down. On my first note, I wrote "beach houses" and on my second note, I wrote "sunrises," because I love mornings.

Two weeks later, an acquaintance mentioned to my husband and I that she knew of a beach house for sale in North Carolina and felt that it was perfect for us. Weeks before, my husband and I were discussing our retirement plans and we were thinking that having a beach house might be fun and suited us. Neither of us knew where Emerald Isle, North Carolina, was, so we searched the location on the Internet, looked at each other and said within five minutes, "Let us buy it!"

Now we have a lovely beach house where we spend our summers watching the sunrise every morning.

Sticky notes are also very handy to help us plan our next day before we go to bed. They help us **build our asking muscle**. This helps us remember what to bring in front of our Heavenly Father the next morning when we have Breakfast with God. The sticky note helps us keep our focus throughout the day.

Let us write the five things we wish to accomplish the next day on a sticky note, pray over the contents, and stick it on the cover of our journal or planner every night before we go to bed. Let us pray over it again in the morning when we wake up and again when we have breakfast. Knock three times!

Chapter 31

THE POWER OF MUSIC

Let us listen to positive music. Music is a language that speaks to our hearts, minds, and souls. Music uplifts the human condition. We are in a beautiful place while harmonious music is playing.

The vibrations of music do affect our vibrational patterns. Our vibrations follow music. When we strike a tuning fork, all tuning forks with the same frequency start to vibrate. When we beat a drumhead, the other drumheads follow the vibration.

The same happens to our body. Our body can vibrate to all frequencies. Our tuning forks are tuned to God. Our hearts adapt to different rhythms and tones. Our heartbeat communicates to our psyche what we feel, thus a fast beat may trigger excitement while a slow, soft beat calms us.

Music can lift our spirit and align our mind with our hearts. Let us listen to music that makes us happy, calms us, and soothes us. Science has proven that sounds can heal as well as the opposite. Let us add "healing frequencies" to our music library and listen to them regularly. These specially crafted sounds, also known as solfeggio frequencies, induce positive effects on the physical body. It readjusts our vibrations and brings them back to their intrinsic state.

Listen to the words of the music. Are they creating beauty and peace? Are they sending positive subliminal messages to our minds? Turn the lyrics around: "You <u>can</u> always *get* what you *want*" and "I <u>can</u> *get* <u>total</u> satisfaction" if we focus on receiving it.

"Speaking to one another with psalms, hymns, and songs from the Spirit. **Sing and make music from your heart to the Lord,**"

—Ephesians 5:19 (NIV)

God desires us to hymn Him. Let us sing praises to Him in church and in our daily lives. Enjoy music as much as possible; visit a live concert or a music festival. Sing in the car, in the shower, with our children, on our walks. If desired, take voice lessons.

"Make a joyful noise to the Lord, all the earth; break forth into joyous song and **sing praises!**"
—Psalm 98:4 (ESV)

Let us play our instruments or pick up a new instrument and take lessons. Music and playing instruments is a theme throughout the Bible. For example, David played the harp (1 Samuel 16:23).

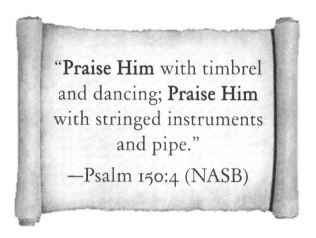

"**Praise Him** with timbrel and dancing; **Praise Him** with stringed instruments and pipe."
—Psalm 150:4 (NASB)

The human heart yearns for beauty—both the beauty in the visible and in the in-visible such as the frequencies of rhythms and words.

Music triggers our mind. It triggers memories and feelings we attached to the memories. We have certain pieces for special occasions: for example, birthday songs, Christmas songs, wedding songs, or favorite music. Music is also inspirational. Music is art. Music is affirming. Listening to a piece over and over makes it easy to remember the lyrics. Let us be conscious of the lyrics that we repeat over and over and anchor in our minds.

Chapter 32

THE POWER OF ANCHORING

Anything we do repetitively anchors in our minds and becomes part of our habitual patterning. Anchoring helps to form new neural pathways. Affirming with words and actions at the same time is the most powerful anchoring. If we speak our affirmations while being physically active as with jogging, tapping, or rebounding, they anchor even deeper.

When using affirmations, the anchoring resonates stronger. Be aware of every word in our affirmations. Every word counts. Please make sure they are entirely positive and beautiful.

Here are examples of affirmations:

- ♥ All is well all the time.

- ♥ There is only happiness. I rejoice always.

- ♥ I allow God's goodness to flow through me.

- ♥ I create miracles in every moment.

- ♥ I ask continually and receive abundantly.

- ♥ I choose to see the good in all.

- ♥ I am a cheerful giver.

- ♥ I am in perfect health. My body feels amazing. All of my cells are happy and healthy.

- ♥ I love myself. I am beautiful.

- ♥ I find it easy to love myself and others.

- ♥ I have faith. I believe. My heart is at peace.

- ♥ My family and friends are loving, kind, helpful, nurturing, and supportive.

- ♥ Wealth continually flows to me. I love being rich. My fun brings all the wealth I desire.

The Power Of Anchoring

Are repetitive affirmations necessary? Only if they make us feel good. If we choose to repeat ourselves 150 times, the first time is for God, the other 149 times are for us. Remember, He hears us perfectly the first time. If we choose to repeat the affirmations in speaking or writing, it helps us feel better ourselves and builds our own confidence.

Anchoring also takes place when we continuously pass our story on. It was about two years ago when a young woman came to see me. Her wish was to be pregnant and become a mother. Up until this point she was only pregnant with her desire to have children.

She asked me if a hormone test was advisable. I asked her what she was seeking as a result of taking the hormone test: "Are you wishing to see that your hormone levels are perfect?" I reminded her that **God advised us to seek and we shall find . . . whatever we seek**. I also asked if all her feelings around being pregnant and having a child were positive.

She thought about it for a while. When she finally answered, she admitted that she lacked faith in her ability to conceive. I asked her with how many people she spoke about it. She admitted that the conversation came up repeatedly with about 10 friends and family members. I then asked her the exact words she used when speaking about this topic. She said,

"I may have *difficulty* having a child." Taking about 10 conversations and repeating them multiple times brought strong focus and anchoring to the "*difficulty*" of having a child. When we repeat the same sentence over and over, we attract the very thing we are talking about repeatedly.

She changed her words and turned her focus on being healthy and able to conceive. Within a few weeks she was pregnant. **As much as clarity and faith, the lack thereof also holds manifestation power.**

Chapter 33

THE POWER OF EXERCISING A CONSCIOUS MIND

Now that we know the steps and helpful tools, let us purify our mind, our body, and our environment.

Observe

Begin with your mind. Be aware of how you use your own mind. Be conscious of your thoughts and words.

To start, for the next two weeks, observe your thoughts and words. Listen to yourself and others. Really pay attention to the words you and the people around you use often and what thought patterns enter your mind regularly.

My desire with this book is to boost your awareness of where your mind is throughout the day and in your dream state. Take the next step while you are consciously observing yourself and ask yourself the following questions:

Do I think positive thoughts all the time?

Do I use only positive words in my vocabulary?

What are the common phrases I use throughout the day?

Are they positive?

What will it take for me to think positive thoughts, speak positive words, and share kindness all the time?

Write

Journal everything and edit your own words three times.

Make two lists, one of what you are grateful for and the other of what you desire. Put one hand on each page and pray over them daily. Pray often.

Plan your day in writing the night before and pray over it.

Have Breakfast with God. Joyfully discuss your day with God.

Improve Your Mind

As you continue to improve your awareness, ask yourself:

How am I feeling?

Am I encouraging myself and others?

Do I read the Bible?

Do I pray on a regular basis?

Do I journal?

Do I use helpful techniques such as meditation, affirmations, and visualization?

Do I have a vision board for my dreams and resolutions?

You may have heard it many times before:

"Do you not know that your **bodies are temples of the Holy Spirit,** who is in you, whom you have received from God? You are not your own."

—1 Corinthians 6:19 (NIV)

Fuel Your Body

Let us praise God and **honor Him by taking care of your temple** *and give the Holy Spirit the glorious vessel it deserves.*

Do I drink enough water?

Do I imprint my water with love and gratitude and all the vibrations I wish to receive?

Do I nourish my physical body with healthy organic food?

Do I bless my food to nourish me before I eat it?

Purify Your Environment

Once your mind and body are taken care of, start to clean up and purify your environment.
Look around your home and work place.
Ask yourself the following questions:

Do I surround myself with only positive, supportive, and encouraging people?

Do I listen to positive music? Will Jesus enjoy the same music I listen to?

Do I create and allow only positive words and phrases around me that encourage me?

Are the magazines, newspapers, and posters I surround myself with encouraging, positive, and aiding in my growth process?

Are the programs I watch on TV using blessed words and encouraging me?

Am I allowing myself to grow?

Am I reading encouraging books and attending seminars of interest to me?

Reach for a Higher Level of Rightmindedness

Continue with passing on your blessings and your uplifting success stories. Another positive thing you can do: Pass this book and positive vibration on to bless someone else.

Go back through this book and do the exercises regularly. With every new reading you welcome in an opportunity for advanced inspiration.

If you wish to educate yourself further, Receive Joy has books and seminars offering more details on this topic.

There is an Ask And You Shall Receive workbook available to practice asking and receiving through heightened awareness and exercises that give you guidance to reach a higher level of rightmindedness.

Stay Focused

Remind yourself:

"I see myself in my total creation package, **asking and receiving** a comfortable, happy, abundant life. Every moment is an exciting opportunity to welcome and investigate my inner being."

Whatever you do, hold on to your dreams. Be true to yourself. This will keep you focused! Stay encouraged. Be joyful. Continuously develop a sense of purpose for your life. Have a mission and a purpose for everything in your life.

The Power Of Exercising A Conscious Mind

Matthew 11:30 promises for the one walking with Jesus and the Holy Spirit,

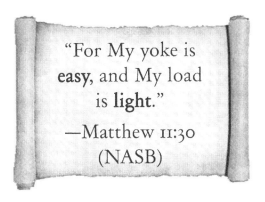

"For My yoke is **easy,** and My load is **light**."

—Matthew 11:30 (NASB)

When our lives are **light and easy** this is when we know that we are yoked to Christ.

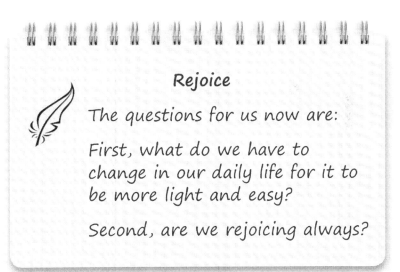

Rejoice

The questions for us now are:

First, what do we have to change in our daily life for it to be more light and easy?

Second, are we rejoicing always?

Let us take 100 percent responsibility for everything in our life. Let us tap into our birthright and use the Nine Step Method. Use the Nine Steps every day all the time! Make it a habit, and most of all let us allow ourselves to **receive joy**! Rejoice always; there is wonderful joy everywhere all the time. All is well.

Chapter 34

LIGHT ONE CANDLE AT A TIME

Everyone can use the Nine Step Method and achieve miraculous creations in their lives. I ask everyone I meet along my path to share their miraculous stories. I also invite all my readers to share their illuminating miracle stories by email.

Our experience on Earth is an opportunity for each of us to investigate our inner being and choose to be a light. My desire is for humanity to **be the light** of love, joy, peace, patience, kindness, goodness, faithfulness, gentleness, and self-control as this is the fruit, the pouring fourth, of the Holy Spirit (Galatians 5:22-23, ESV).

My wish is for each of us to **be a conscious light** so that we can **light others**, one candle (person) at a time. Let us be conscious of our thoughts and our words. Let us be rightminded so that our light of truth is whole and well as it flows through us and is passed on.

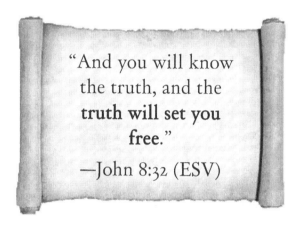

"And you will know the truth, and the **truth will set you free.**"

—John 8:32 (ESV)

REDISCOVER TRUTH and

Receive Joy

ASK AND YOU SHALL RECEIVE

> "**Ask**, and it will be given to you;
> **seek** and you will find; **knock** and
> the door will be opened to you.
> For everyone who asks receives;
> the one who seeks finds; and to
> the one who knocks, the door
> will be opened."
>
> —Matthew 7:7-8 (NIV)

We live in a Quantum World where the divine delivery system is free and there is more than enough of everything for everyone. This is the truth of the Universe. What we think about most, we attract. Let us gain consciousness of our thoughts and focus on what we do desire. Let us ask only for what we do desire in exact detail. Let us imprint our Morphic Field with our goals: write them down and edit them three times. **Ask, ask, ask**, and allow ourselves to **receive**. Give freely. Water is imprintable and so are we. Use only blessed positive words and our good deeds will follow. The mind attracts, the word creates. Our emotions enhance our co-creation power. Let us listen to our inner guidance system. Let us start new in every moment. Knock three times: Think it, speak it, and write it down.

The Nine Steps To Conscious Creation

1. **Connect**: Plug into God's Almighty **Gift**, the Power of the Universe, and discover your life's purpose.

2. **Declare**: Be clear about what you are truly seeking and ask for it.
Have **Faith,** focus, and be courageous.

3. **Dominate**: Receive your inheritance and put on your crown.
Believe.

4. **Be calm**: **Align** your head with your heart.
Have **Peace**.

5. **Take action**: Focus on your breath and let the "how" be up to God.
Let Him wow us with the "how." He does it.

6. **Lead with love**: Let us **love ourselves first**.
Have **Grace**.

7. **Bless everyone** and **everything** with **love and gratitude.**
Have **Mercy**.

8. **Expect the miracle in every moment.** Know the **Truth**.
Be conscious of what you create and allow yourself to receive your desires.

9. **Have fun and celebrate**: Enjoy your creation and rejoice.
Trust God.

Let us:

♥ Use the Nine Step Method

♥ Be conscious in our practice:

       Have a Five Minute Couch Time

       Make everything a Ten Star Experience

       Build our Supernatural Ship

♥ Pray often

♥ Attend a Miracle Group

♥ Start journaling: create a Receive Joy Journal and use it every day

♥ Practice daily meditation

♥ Use visualization:

       Create a vision board

       Have Breakfast with God and bring our five daily desires before Him with the easy help of a sticky note

♥ Listen to positive music

♥ Use the Power of anchoring

♥ Exercise a conscious mind:

       Observe

       Write

       Improve our mind

       Fuel our body

       Purify our environment

       Reach for a higher level of rightmindedness

       Stay focused

       Rejoice and play the game Life of Fun

- ♥ Light one candle at a time
- ♥ Love and Pray Through Our Life
- ♥ Rediscover Truth

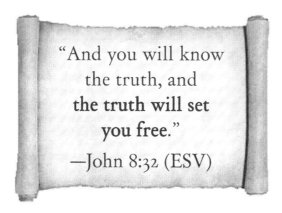

"And you will know the truth, and **the truth will set you free.**"
—John 8:32 (ESV)

Let us enjoy ourselves as a new and more powerful, focused and loved, aware and connected, **light and easy** being!

ASK AND YOU SHALL RECEIVE

Receive Joy

Rediscover Truth

(239) 450-1240
ask@receivejoy.com
www.receivejoy.com

THE STORY BEHIND THE BOOK COVER

Rece and Ive Joy created the book cover on one special day. It was a Tuesday and we were on the way to visit a dear friend. She had invited us to come to a gathering for a new charity—The Genesis Project. Her friend Deborah W. Maurer invited local leaders to a round-table discussion to explore possibilities of how to help the community most. She had a great vision in mind and welcomed input from professionals in various fields.

It was a four-hour drive for us. On the way to our friend we stopped at the home of a graphic designer who was recommended to us the day before. We explained to him our vision for our logo and our book cover. This meeting was so fruitful that we walked out with our beautiful logo and the font for our book cover.

Our logo is inspired from the complementary frequencies of giving and receiving as well as flowing and allowing. It also represents the vibrational ripple effect of water and the waves that transport information.

It was a sheer pleasure to see our friend and we met so many great, interesting people during the gathering. Afterward we stayed with our friend and Deborah to help clean up and we started a loving conversation. She explained to us how she received her charity vision and her calling from God.

She showed us a beautiful picture of an angel formed from clouds in the sky and told us the story behind it:

"After God called me, everything changed. God asked me to be a voice for love. I went by myself to St. Augustine, Florida, for the 10th annual 'March for Life.' When I arrived, I felt alone. I sat down wondering, 'Why was I here?' My ego inside said, 'Just go home.' I asked God, 'God, please give me a sign and I will stay. Is there anything I can do here?'

"I looked up in the sky and there it was: an angel standing on the sextant navigating the stars to the crescent moon. I immediately submitted and decided to walk in His way."

Deborah W. Maurer graciously allowed us to use her beautiful picture.

thegenesisprojectcenter@gmail.com

ACKNOWLEDGMENTS

With Love and Gratitude, we give our heartfelt thanks to the following:

- ♥ God, Jesus, and the Holy Spirit for guiding us with your inspiration and content of this book.

- ♥ Ourselves for our dedicated focus and love to complete the book for all humanity.

- ♥ Our families and friends for their ongoing love.

- ♥ Everyone in our Miracle Group: All the beautiful, positive people who shared their joy and their creation stories and who always are a delight to be around.

- ♥ Deborah W. Maurer for the use of her beautiful angel picture.

Ask And You Shall Receive

♥ Tom Messina for the amazing graphic design and his help to bring our visions of a logo and book cover into the digital dimension.

♥ Christine Perry, Karen B. Barnett, Carol Fitzgerald, Kathryn Gaertner, Lisa Delfin, and Barbara Compagnucci.

♥ Our beloved editor Joey Madia and our amazing textual editor Harriet Howard Heithaus.

♥ James Subramanian for making a beautiful book out of a manuscript.

♥ And everyone we met along the journey of writing Ask And You Shall Receive.

READING RECOMMENDATION

THE BEAUTIFUL WORD SOLUTION

by Kathryn Gaertner

(CreateSpace Independent Publishing Platform; 2017)

Receive joy, positivity, and beauty. Let us help you sustain patterns of love and gratitude. Enjoy more fun, laughter, light-heartedness, ease, and flow in your daily experience.

In the book *"The Beautiful Word Solution"* you will learn to use written prayer processes. With beautiful words, these prayer processes will maintain your vibrational tone in positive focus.

Beautiful words leverage our well-being. They buoy our positive emotions. They augment our appreciation of the life we are designing, the world we live in and the people we love. They focus our pathway into beauty.

Faith is a choice. I choose to see beauty everywhere and enjoy beauty every day. Our beautiful words are the bridge into our glorious future.

Made in the USA
Columbia, SC
25 November 2017